Metaphysics

Charles A. Baylis
DUKE UNIVERSITY

Sources in Philosophy

A MACMILLAN SERIES
Lewis White Beck, General Editor
THE MACMILLAN COMPANY, NEW YORK
COLLIER–MACMILLAN LIMITED, LONDON

To my teachers who directed my thinking,
To my colleagues and students who sharpened it, and
To my readers in the hope that they will learn from it.

Contents

Introduction

Philosophers have discussed such widely variant topics under the broad heading "Metaphysics" that it is difficult to formulate a definition applicable to the many diverse usages of the term. "Metaphysics," it is believed, was first used about 70 B.C., when it was applied to certain of Aristotle's work written after his discussions of *Physics;* thus the term carried the minimal import of "after *Physics.*" But this statement throws little light on the subject matter of metaphysics.

Aristotle describes what he treated under "Metaphysics" as "the science of being as such"[1] and distinguishes it from studies of specialized kinds of being—from those studies, for example, referred to today as "the natural sciences." Guided by Aristotle, some writers think of metaphysics as a study of completely general first principles and regard the sciences of today as in some sense a spelling out of truths that apply only to limited kinds of things, for example, physical things, chemical things, living things, and the like. That the empirical methods of today's sciences are very different from the meditative insights of Aristotle about the nature of things of any kind whatever is quite consistent with Aristotle's view that detailed observation and induction are the necessary first steps in the acquisition of knowledge, even though that knowledge is ultimately ordered by deductive relations between metaphysical first principles and specific scientific details.

The problems of metaphysics have been described quite differently by F. H. Bradley and others who regard them as being concerned with the nature of "Reality" and its distinction from appearance. Are relations, for example, real? A not unrelated question is advanced by metaphysicians who ask "Is matter real?" or "Is mind real?"

An alternative way of describing metaphysics is to say that it consists of knowledge organized and systematized by the use of those broad and basic categories or concepts that have the widest and most fundamental applications. According to this approach, the central task of metaphysics is the critical study and organization of key concepts, a task often given the name "categorial analysis." Rudolf Carnap[2] has urged that *within* any such systematic framework of basic concepts, questions such as "What are the properties of

---

[1] *Metaphysics,* Gamma, 2a11.

[2] Rudolf Carnap, "Empiricism, Semantics and Ontology," *Revue Internationale de Philosophie,* **IV** (1950), pp. 20–40.

plutonium?" or "Are whales mammals?" are answerable by common sense or empirical science. He asserts, however, that *external* questions *about* such basic categories or their systematic relations, are neither true nor false but are inquiries about the utility of using such a conceptual framework for organizing and describing our experience.

Bradley's type of questions and Carnap's meet in such queries as: "Do we need relations which are so complex that they bind everything in the universe into a tight coherent system?" Other writers urge as the important task of metaphysics a thorough re-examination and perhaps quite radical revision of extant systems of categories.

Even this sketchy account of some of the diverse views that have been held about metaphysics suggests that we would do well to postpone theorizing about "the nature of metaphysics" until we have examined an array of different metaphysical problems. Seeing how such problems arise, how they are formulated, the various answers proposed to them, the arguments offered for one solution or another, and so on, will prove invaluable for understanding metaphysics, its methods, and the values of the results thus far achieved.

I. THE ULTIMATE NATURE OF REALITY

Many metaphysicians have been concerned primarily with some such question as: "What is the nature of the ultimate substance or stuff or content of which everything in the universe is composed?" Or, if they have believed that there is more than one such ultimate substance, they have asked: "What is the nature of each different kind?"

Thus materialists have said: "All is matter"—sometimes adding with a twinkle, "never mind." Idealists, on the other hand, have allegedly asserted: "All is mind, no matter." Realists agree that there are two basic substances, one mental and the other material. We examine these views in turn.

1. *Materialism: Does the universe consist exclusively of matter and energy?* The first Western philosopher, Thales (*circa* 600 B.C.), asked a question philosophers ever since have been trying to answer. "What is the ultimate nature of reality?" A recurrent type of answer has been that of materialism: Everything is of the nature of matter or energy. Even consciousness is reducible to matter and physical energy.

The rise and rapid development first of animal psychology and then, especially, of behavioristic psychology in the early years of the twentieth century gave materialism new support. Research and theorizing in these areas seemed to many to point directly to a thoroughly materialistic account of mind and mental events. It was noted first that many so-called mental occurrences were correlated with accompanying physical changes in the body. In the higher mammals, including *homo sapiens,* sensation and perception occur only when some sense-organ of the perceiving body is stimulated, causing changes in its nervous system. Researchers established that damage to certain areas of the brain interferes with vision, damage to other areas impairs muscular control of an arm or leg, and so on. It was a simple inductive inference that every so-called mental event had its physiological correlate of bodily and neural change. Only one more leap was required to reach the conclusion that the "mental" event was caused by or was identical with the correlated physical change.

It was noted, for example, that an emotion such as anger has regular physiological accompaniments—increased heart beat and respiration, clenching of the hands, flushing of the face, release of sugar into the blood and of adrenaline from the adrenal gland, and the like. Such facts led to the James-Lange theory of emotions, the theory "that the bodily changes follow directly the perception of the existing fact, and that our feeling of the same changes as they occur *is* the emotion . . . that we feel sorry because we cry, angry because we strike, afraid because we tremble, and not that we cry, strike or tremble, because we are sorry, angry, or fearful, as the case may be." [3] This is often taken to imply that physical changes are either the causes of or are identical with consciously felt emotions.

Contemporary behavioristic psychologists, it is sometimes said, fall into two classes, the "mild" ones who assert that physical changes accompany and have some causal relationship with all mental events, and the "wild" ones who assert that mental events are nothing but these physical changes. The evidence for both views is the same, namely the apparent constant conjunction between events of the two kinds. Only the latter qualifies as strict materialism. "Mild" behaviorists hold at most that mind is completely dependent on body, that mental events always result from· physical ones. This approach, called "epiphenomenalism," is just one of several possible views about the relation between mind and body.

[3] William James, *Psychology* (Briefer course; New York: Henry Holt & Co., 1920), p. 375.

According to another position, "interactionism," the two interact. Sometimes a depressing thought will lower one's heart beat; sometimes a decreasing heart beat will cause a mental depression. This view is so widely accepted that it has markedly infected our language. We commonly speak of physical causes for certain mental illnesses, but we have learned also to speak of psychosomatic disorders, which seems to imply causation in the other direction. Another approach to the body-mind relationship, one encountered in the works of Spinoza, is "parallelism," according to which a human being has both physical and mental characteristics. A complete parallelist would hold that these are so closely connected, any change in either being accompanied by a change in the other, that we can properly regard them as co-relative aspects of the same thing. The analogy of a curved line with a convex side and a concave side has often been used. There is never either without the other.

The existence of these plausible alternatives to a strict materialism does much to weaken the case for that view. At most the evidence indicates some relationship between mental and physical characteristics or occurrences. This might be a causal relation from brain to mind or from mind to brain, an interactionistic one, with causal relations sometimes in one, sometimes in the other, direction, or a parallelistic relationship without causal efficacy. But one thing is sure: If this relationship is causal or concomitant between distinct changes it cannot be a relationship of identity. No cause could ever be identical with its effect, for it has characteristics that its effect lacks, for example, preceding the latter in time.

An empirical type of argument is also used to deny the identity of mental and physical concomitants. There seem to be some mental events or characteristics that have characteristics that are not possessed by any physical event or characteristic. For example, a person may be clearly aware of his intentions for a given evening and not at all aware of their physical correlates. Physical occurrences have one set of characteristics, mental intentions quite a different set. This sort of empirical evidence seems to weigh against a strict materialism, though it leaves open the epiphenomenalistic view which asserts not that matter—or matter and energy—alone exists, but rather that only matter is causally efficacious. Such a view is consistent with a naturalism which holds that only material causal factors exist.

2. *Idealism: Is everything ultimately of the nature of mind?* The principal arguments for the view that everything is mental were offered by George Berkeley, later Bishop of Cloyne, in *The Principles*

of Human Knowledge (1710) and *Three Dialogues Between Hylas and Philonous* (1713). His position, often called "subjective ideal-ism" (see the Berkeley selection, "Idealism"), begins with a statement as to what things we know. Subjectively, he says, we know ourselves. We are immediately conscious of ourselves, of that which senses, perceives, knows, acts, wills, and so on. This, he says, is myself, my mind, my spirit, my soul. Objectively, we know ideas, which are of two kinds, sensations and mental images. Sensations are presented to our knowing minds, as it were, from outside, and are independent of our own volition. They are strong, steady, distinct, and coherent. Mental images are sensory images; whether of dreams, memory, or imagination they are pretty much controlled by us, and are weak and lack in vividness and coherence. For example, my present visual image of the Paris Opera was called up by me after an auditory image of the opening bars of Gounod's *Faust* and is quite vague. These criteria, of vividness, uncontrollability, and coherence, are still the chief grounds available to a perceiver for distinguishing sensations from images.

Thus far in his account, Berkeley agrees largely with the views of his predecessors, Descartes and Locke. But at this point he differs. Descartes and Locke both hold that there exists also an external world which is the cause of or like the sensations a perceiver has, but Berkeley denies this. Spirits and their ideas alone exist. Tables and apples and mountains do indeed exist but only as ideas in some mind.

Surprising, even shocking, as this view first appears, Berkeley musters four good arguments for it:

1. If we examine a material object, say a piece of chalk, what we find are a number of sensations or sense qualities; for example, whiteness, hardness, a certain feel, a certain odor, a certain taste. And these are all we directly sense. If we believe that there is more than this before us, our belief is based on inference, an inference that seems to Berkeley thoroughly unjustifiable.

2. The view of Descartes and Locke with regard to secondary qualities, roughly those observable through not more than one sense, for example, the sense qualities of color, odor, taste, sound, touch, and the like, coincides with Berkeley's. Such qualities exist only in the mind. Descartes and Locke, however, maintain that their occur-rence in mind is due to primary qualities—those observable by more than one sense, for example, shape, size, mass, motion, and the like—which really exist in an external object. All three writers agree in

basing their denial of the real existence of secondary qualities apart from minds on the well-known relativity of these qualities to the individual perceiver. The same physical object can be seen to have one color by one person, and quite a different color by another. A sound can be heard as loud by one person, soft by another. And so on through the list of secondary qualities. Primary qualities of objects, however, Locke and Descartes hold, do not share the relativity exhibited by secondary qualities, and hence, there really are objects that have primary qualities independent of this or that or indeed any perceiver. Berkeley, however, staunchly denies this and argues that primary qualities are just as relative to the particular perceiver as are secondary qualities. What shape does the top of a desk seem visually to have? Doesn't this depend on the point of view of the observer? Or, consider motion. If you are sitting in a train between two other trains and one of the three moves, which one is it that is moving? Hard to tell, isn't it? Motion is notoriously relative. Even if we ascertain that the train we are in is not moving relative to the station, we agree that it is moving relative to the north star. We may safely conclude, Berkeley urges, that primary qualities are fully as relative as secondary ones, and if relativity to the perceiver is a sign, as Locke and Descartes take it to be, of dependence at least in part on the perceiver, then primary qualities, too, are dependent on the perceiver and vary with different perceivers. But what do we ever sense about so-called material objects except sense qualities, primary or secondary? These qualities, since they depend on the mind of the perceiver, are mind-dependent; Berkeley concludes that they do not exist independently of mind as part of an external, independent world.

3. The argument against the independent reality of material objects that Berkeley seems to regard as most devastating is, however, the one R. B. Perry happily baptized (many years later) as "the argument from the ego-centric predicament." This predicament is not itself a theory or an argument; it is a fact. No one has ever sensed anything he did not sense, nor thought of anything he did not think of. To be sure, we are tempted to reply, can I not think of the desk in my office when I am at home and not sensing it? Of course, Berkeley replies, you are not sensing it then, but are you not, by your own confession, thinking of it? You cannot think of anything you are not thinking of. Thus Berkeley concludes that since we cannot sense anything that is not being sensed by a mind and cannot think of anything that is not being thought of by a mind,

therefore nothing exists that is not either sensed or thought of by a mind. Thus, using "perceived" as the equivalent of "either sensed or thought of" it follows that *to be is to be perceived. Esse est percipi.* At least this is true as far as physical objects are concerned. They consist of bundles of qualities each of which is an idea dependent on a mind.

4. Berkeley's fourth argument is a defensive one in which he argues against the assumption, which Descartes and Locke and others had taken for granted, that every physical object is composed of the material substance, matter, and that it is this matter that has the qualities we are able to perceive, sense, or think of. Berkeley asks what reason we could possibly have for believing that there is such a thing as a material substance. By their own account Descartes and Locke agree that no one ever does or can sense it. Let us stick to the evidence of our senses, Berkeley urges; let us abstain from wild metaphysical speculation. Why not stick to what we know? We know only minds and the ideas minds have. Let us retain our initial maxim: to be is either to be an idea or to be a mind which has an idea. To be is to be perceived or to be a perceiver. Further, argues Berkeley, even if we were to grant to believers in material substance that matter exists, this would not at all help us to understand how we come to sense any sense quality. Suppose we try to accept the usual account given by believers in matter and say that the material object affects our material bodies through our material sense organs and material nerves until finally there is a change in the cortex of our material brains. And then, *mirabile dictu,* we sense a sense quality. But would you kindly, asks Berkeley, explain this last step in the process. How could this mysterious and unobservable material substance that is totally unlike a mind bring it about that a mind should have an idea, whether a sensation or an image? Why should we accept this completely unobserved and unobservable hypothetical entity, a material substance, when such a supposition has no explanatory power whatever in accounting for our ideas?

Moreover, and here Berkeley turns to his own view for a positive account, we do know how a mind can give itself one class of ideas, namely those we call images. If we have had a sensation of red, we can imagine that same shade of red, and so also for any other sense quality. We know then that a mind can give itself one kind of ideas, namely images. But how do we come to have the originals for these images, that is, sensations? We know that we do not give ourselves sensations, for they are out of our control. They come to all men in a very regular fashion, according, as we say, to the Laws of Nature. If we suppose that just as a mind can create images it must also be possible for a mind to create sensations, we must take into account that a mind that can give us such regular and coherent sensations must be much more comprehensive, powerful, and systematic than ourselves. Who, then, but God, could be the source of our sensations? God gives us sensations as we give ourselves images, but he gives them to us in a regular fashion. The Laws of Nature are the thoughts of God. Furthermore, God perceives these sensations when no human being does. God perceived this earth when there were no human beings on it.

What should we conclude about this striking metaphysical view of Berkeley? To be real is to be of the nature of mind; it is to be either a mind or an idea in a mind. No unprejudiced reader of Berkeley can fail to realize that he develops a plausible and interesting case for his view. He makes a number of minor errors, but these he could probably have corrected fairly easily. Aside from them he appears to present a view that is free from logical contradictions and is therefore possible. Are his arguments for his view coercive? Is any reasonable man forced to accept a Berkeleyan type of metaphysics? I think not. This conclusion is justified by a critical look at each of his three positive arguments:

1'. Berkeley's argument, that we never observe anything but sensations and that these are mental, loses its force as soon as we make the distinction that Bertrand Russell and others have insisted on, that between the act or process of sensing and that which is sensed. Even if the former is a mental act or process, it does not follow that what is sensed—that sense-quality, or the sense-datum, as it has often been called—is itself mental or mind dependent. A color quality, for example, is indeed the sort of entity a mind is capable of sensing, but it does not follow that it is itself mental or that its existence is dependent on its being sensed. For a perceiver to become aware of a sense-datum it must be sensed by him, but it does not follow from this that for a sense-datum to be, to exist, a perceiver must be conscious of it. To observe microbes one needs a microscope, but we do not jump to the conclusion that microbes can not exist without a microscope.

2'. But does not the relativity of sense qualities to the nature of the observer and the intervening medium, and so on, show that they are dependent upon him and the medium, and so on, either for their existence or for their nature? This conclusion, while possible, is far from being necessary. It is indeed a fact that different people report the color of a given piece of cloth, for example, quite differently. One says it is bluish, another that it is greenish, another that it is turquoise-like. One can indeed entertain the hypothesis that it has none of these colors, but that in each case a color is present in the perceiver's mind and he erroneously attributes it to the object. Or one can say that the cloth really has all the colors it can be seen to have—it at least has the *potentiality* of being seen to have all of these colors—but that which of its many colors it is seen to have by a given individual depends on such factors as the nature of that individual's eyes, the nature of the lighting, and the nature of the intervening medium. Or one can take the more common view and hold that the object itself has only one color and that to perceive it an observer must have eyes and nerves of a certain sort and must observe the object under something like standard conditions of lighting and intervening medium. Any relevant difference in light, medium, or observer may cause him to misperceive the actual color of the object. This latter account not only is the common-sense one but also is backed by common scientific procedures which identify colors in terms both of the frequencies of the transmitting light rays and of the colors then observed by "standard"-eyed perceivers.

3′. The argument from the ego-centric predicament, unlike the predicament itself, which is a fact, is fallacious, as has often been pointed out. It simply does not follow logically from the fact that a certain process is necessary for something to be perceived that the existence or nature of what is perceived is dependent on the perceiving process. Rather, the most that could justifiably be inferred would seem to be that only if the object were of a certain kind *could it be perceived* by an individual whose perceptual powers limit him to perceiving objects of that kind. Thus a red-green color-blind person cannot perceive those colors correctly. If everyone were red-green color blind, we might not *know* that there are red or green colors, but it would not *follow* that they do not exist.

The conclusion that seems to be indicated by this examination of Berkeleyan idealism is that though it is a possible view there are no coercive reasons for accepting it. Against accepting it are the following considerations: (1) The extent to which Berkeley falls back on the unproved assumption of God to account for the cause of human sensations and for their continued existence when they are not sensed by human beings. (2) The apparently much greater simplicity of the realistic view that sensations are due to stimulation by material objects that exist whether sensed or not. (3) The ease with which subjective idealism slips into the very questionable view called "solipsism." This is the view of a person who holds that "I and my ideas alone exist." [4] It arises from subjective idealism by a person's noting that the only self he is directly acquainted with is his own self and the only ideas he directly knows are his own ideas. The general trend that idealism has taken is in the opposite direction toward absolutism. (See section 4 below.)

3. *Realism: Are there two distinct substances, mind and matter?* Departing from the monistic metaphysical doctrines of materialism and idealism, many philosophers turn to a view that seems much closer to common sense. According to this view, called "realism," there exist two substances, matter and mind. Either may exist independently, matter in mountains, for example, and minds in angels or other spiritual beings. But in human beings, realists generally hold, they are closely interrelated.

As noted earlier, either parallelism or epiphenomenalism [5] or interactionism may be true. By far the most common view is that mind and matter, though each a distinct substance, interact. Minds affect bodies and bodies affect minds. Needless to say, though these alternatives all seem logically possible, no coercive evidence seems ever to have been offered for preferring one of these views to the exclusion of its alternatives.

Of very much more interest to philosophers have been questions asking how minds are able to perceive bodies, as they apparently do. Here again many possible answers have been proposed, but the two most famous ones have been (1) representative realism and (2) presentative realism. The former view goes back at least to Descartes and Locke. According to this view physical objects have primary qualities but do not have the secondary qualities we sense. In veridical perception our minds have ideas of primary qualities that match the qualities of the perceived physical object. Where there are no such matching qualities, we are suffering from illusion or hallucination. In

---

[4] It is sometimes expressed as "My ideas alone exist" or "The world is my idea (or the set of my ideas)."

[5] It is logically possible to hold a view that is the opposite of this, namely that material substance is entirely dependent on mental substance and subordinate to it, but holders of such a view are few and far between if indeed there are any at all.

the case of secondary qualities, these—or rather ideas of them—exist only in the mind, for material objects have no sensible secondary qualities. They do have, however, at least according to Locke, certain powers or capacities to cause a perceiver to have ideas of secondary qualities. Where such powers are operating effectively our ideas of these secondary qualities are justified in a way they are not when they are not so produced. Our knowledge of material objects is thus entirely representative in character. When ideas are correctly representative, we have knowledge, otherwise error. Obviously one serious difficulty facing this type of view is concerned with trying to explain how we can ever know that our ideas of primary qualities correspond with the primary qualities of the perceived object and how we can ever know that our ideas of secondary qualities related to that object are justified. An excellent defense of representative realism of this kind is offered by Arthur O. Lovejoy in his book, *The Revolt Against Dualism.*

According to presentative realism, on the other hand, the fundamental error of the representative realists is to think of the mind as something like a camera which has some good pictures in it of primary qualities and some bad ones. If we can escape from this misleading figure of speech, presentative realists urge, we can find a much more apt one in thinking of a mind as analogous to a searchlight. When a material object falls within the rays of a mind's perceptual searchlight, that mind becomes directly aware of that object and of many of its qualities and properties. Having examined that object to our satisfaction, we can then turn the rays of our mind's searchlight onto another object. The object we are no longer perceiving continues to exist and retains nearly all of the characteristics we have just finished perceiving it to have. But now we are becoming aware of the characteristics that the new object we are perceiving has. If we are careful, we need make no perceptual mistake, for the object we seek to perceive is there before us and open to scrutiny by means of our perceptual apparatus.

Representative realists have been quick to ask presentative realists to explain how error is possible according to their view. Accounting for knowledge may be difficult for representationalists, but accounting for error where the perceived object is directly before us for examination seems to present at least an equal problem to the presentationalists. Many such realists have indeed failed this question badly, but some are now seeking—and finding—explanations in terms of misperceiving that is due either to peculiarities of the perceptual situation or to defects in the physiological apparatus involved in perception. Such writers as Gilbert Ryle, Wilfrid Sellars, and the author have been working at this.

An entirely different type of account of perception, in terms of sense-data, was often undertaken during the first half of this century. Bertrand Russell, C. D. Broad, H. H. Price, and others have all advanced views according to which we can and often do sense sense-qualities quite correctly. According to some views these sense-data are themselves parts of, or aspects of, or characters of the physical object perceived, or of the surface of that object. Or, on another type of sense-data theory, they are members of a class of sense data which is that object (see the Russell selection). On representative theories sense-data are at best but signs of properties of objects. For these and other variations on a sense-datum account the best that can be done here is to suggest references for further reading.[6]

4. *Absolutism: Is everything in the universe a supraorganic unity?* Absolutism is a very different kind of metaphysical view. It is concerned less with questions about the number and basically different kinds of substance there are than with queries about the interrelations of whatever entities there are, whether they be material or mental or both or neither. Are the entities or things that exist more or less independent of each other, or are they very closely related so that everything is intimately bound up with everything else, with the resulting whole forming a unity, or absolute, of the most closely knit kind? Absolutists hold that the latter is the case. Some go so far as to insist that these interrelations are so complex that everything is bound into a superorganic unity in which any change in anything would change everything about everything.

In its simplest form absolutism is an elaboration of Tennyson's poem about the flower in the crannied wall. If only we knew all about it we should know all about all. The reason given is that everything is internally related to everything else, makes a difference to everything else as everything else does to it, and so on. To know all about a flower one would have to know, for instance, about the ground out of which it grew, the moisture and natural nourishment on which it thrived, the effect on it of the changing seasons, the sunshine and clouds, and so on. And of course these matters are related to everything in the universe, gravitationally, spatially, tem-

---

[6] Bertrand Russell, *Our Knowledge of the External World* (Chicago: Open Court Publishing Co., 1914), Chaps. 3, 4. Cf. also Bibliography.

porally, and so on. Every component of the universe is so closely related to every other that nothing could be different without everything being different. This theory of the internality of relations leads to the conclusion that to think of the universe properly we should conceive of it as a single unity, The Absolute. If anything were different, everything would be; if we knew all about anything, we would know all about everything.

This type of view has been developed in many different forms by a large number of writers. Among these are Georg W. F. Hegel (1807), F. H. Bradley (1891), Josiah Royce (1900), H. H. Joachim (1906), J. M. E. McTaggart (1921), and Brand Blanshard (1940). Although all these writers agree that everything is united in a single, all-embracing complex unity, they, and other absolutists disagree among themselves as to the nature of this absolute. Some think of it as an absolute self, a mind. Others think of it as psychophysical in nature, having both mental and physical attributes, a view not unlike Spinoza's pantheism. It would be possible for a materialist to be an absolutist as well, holding that all matter and energy are united into an absolute whole. Many idealists have combined the absolutistic motif with their idealism and have concluded that reality is both mental and an absolute unity, either an absolute idea or an absolute mind. This type of view is usually called "absolute idealism." Most of the writers mentioned earlier in this paragraph tend to be classified as holding some form of it. What unifies these quite different views is the inclusion in all of them of some form of "the internality of relations."

Even this common doctrine has been expressed in many different forms. F. H. Bradley expresses it, "Every relation essentially penetrates the being of its terms and is in this sense *intrinsical.*" [7] Blanshard puts it even more strongly by asserting "I follow Joachim in holding that in a perfectly coherent system every proposition would entail all others, if only for the reason that its meaning could never be fully understood without apprehension of the system in its entirety." [8] A critical analysis of the argument for absolutism is given in the Baylis selection (pp. 55).

One difficulty in asserting absolutism arises from the many different ways in which the doctrine of the internality of relations has been expressed. Of the many ways in which it has been interpreted, two stand out in striking contrast: (1) Any change in any

---

[7] *Appearance and Reality* (London: George Allen & Unwin Ltd., 1925), p. 392.

[8] *The Nature of Thought* (New York, The Macmillan Co., 1940), Vol. 2, p. 266, footnote.

character of anything entails changes in some characters of all things. (2) Any change of any character of anything entails changes in all the characters of all things. I have urged (see the Baylis selection) that (1) is true but does not suffice to prove absolutism, whereas (2), which does provide the complete interrelatedness required by that doctrine, is false.

II. BASIC CATEGORIES

Thus far, it has been assumed that the universe consists of particular, individual, existing things or substances, mental or physical, or both (or perhaps neither), each of which has many characteristics, that is, qualities, properties, or relations. The particulars which are somewhat like Aristotle's "first principles" (see the Aristotle selection), have characteristics but could not themselves characterize anything. Characteristics do characterize and in turn have characteristics of their own. This seems at first glance straightforward enough, but serious problems have arisen about both particulars and characteristics.

5. *Substance.* (A) *Must a substance have characteristics?* An initial problem seems to arise in trying to distinguish between a substance and its characteristics. To begin with let us agree that nothing exists that has no characteristics. There is no such thing as a *bare* substance, a characterless something. Yet philosophers have written commonly of characteristics and of *that which* has characteristics. If we ask about the nature of a particular substance, the answer can only be given by reference to its characteristics. But if we try to think of that which has these characteristics as it would be if it had none, we have no intelligible way of referring to what we are talking about. What we need to say is rather something like this: To exist is to have characteristics. Nothing exists completely sans characteristics. Particulars, that is substances, have characteristics and so also do characteristics. In this respect they are alike. But they differ in that a characteristic is precisely the sort of entity that characterizes something or other whereas a particular is precisely the sort of entity that could not possibly characterize anything.

The notion of a bare substance with no characteristics whatsoever has often been referred to as the concept of a "substratum," and it has then promptly been denied that there are any substrata. This seems to be correct, for to be or to exist is to have characteristics. What then is a substance? A substance is an entity that (a) always has characteristics and (b) cannot characterize. It is distinguished from characteristics by requirement (b); it is distinguished from instances of substrata if, per impossible, there were any, by having characteristics and by existing; whereas there are no substrata, there are substances, for example, this book, this man, and so on. What is referred to by the term substance (as it is here used) is always then something with characteristics.

(B) *What distinguishes one substance from another?* The usual answer to this question seems at first blush obvious. One particular thing or substance is distinguished from all others by having a set of characteristics which nothing else has. This answer was formulated by Leibniz in his famous principle of The Identity of Indiscernibles, sometimes named more accurately "The Difference of the Diverse": There cannot be diversity without difference in some respect. Leibniz states the matter this way: "It is not possible for two individuals to exist entirely alike or different only numerically. . . ." [9]

A natural first attempt to criticize this doctrine is to suggest that it seems *logically* possible for there to be two physical objects, say two peas in a pod that are exactly alike, same size, same texture, and so on. Leibniz would reply by calling attention to the different histories of their development. But one can then ask, is it not *logically possible* for there to be two objects exactly alike in all respects including their historical development? Most critics of the principle seem ready enough to admit that in the actual world there are no two things alike in all of their characteristics, but they ask why there *could* not be (or could not have been) a world in which two things are (were) thus alike. To this query it is frequently replied that even in that case they would differ in their spatiotemporal characteristics, that is, in their spatial or temporal relations to other things.

But modern theories of spatiotemporal relativity require that spatial or temporal differences can be specified only by the different relations of otherwise individuated objects or events to one another. Objects or events are in this sense logically prior to spatial or temporal locations. Therefore some such objects must be in-

---

[9] From Leibniz' "Remarks on the letter of M. Arnaud touching on my proposition: that the individual notion of each person includes once for all everything that will ever happen to him," in a letter to Hessen-Rheinfels, May, 1686. The translation here is done by C. A. Baylis from the French original as published in *Philosophischen Schriften,* ed. by C. J. Gebhardt (Berlin, 1879), Vol. ii, p. 42.

dividuated and identifiable to serve as a reference frame in terms of which spatial or temporal relations can be specified (see the Black selection).

If some such line of argument is sound then neither qualitative nor spatiotemporal differences will suffice for individuating particulars. But what then does individuate? To answer, as some philosophers have done, by saying that each particular is differentiated from all others, no matter how completely it is like them, by its haecceity, by its "thisness," is but to give a name to our ignorance. Here then seems to be an unsolved problem upon which metaphysicians can continue to sharpen their wits.

6. *Universals, that is, Characters.* (A) *What distinguishes a character from a substance?* Suppose that we want to describe a table. Of course, by calling it a "table," we have already said some things about it; we have said that it is a table and have implied, for instance, that it has a reasonably flat top and is supported by something in the way of legs. But what shape is the top? What color? How many legs are there? What is their shape? What are they made of? Is this table larger or smaller than that table?, and so forth. Our answers to questions of this sort consist of attributing to the table various qualities, properties, and relations. Let us use the general term "character" of any quality, property, or relation of which we can conceive, without implying by the use of that term either that this character has been conceived or that something actually has it.

This is substituting the term "character" for the more classical term "universal." But the latter term has at least two disadvantages that are worth avoiding; it has been used, by Aristotle and other logicians, to distinguish also a special class of propositions, those about all things of a certain kind or about no things of that kind, for example, "All crows are black" and "No living Texan is twelve feet tall." This usage is very different from the one we want here. Second, the term "universal" has been so long discussed and so vehemently that fixed positions about the various problems concerned have been firmly adopted. Hence, for many philosophers, to suggest a different view is like waving a red rag before a bull. We will therefore use the term "character" for any quality, property, or relation, for example, sphericity, which any particular thing might have or fail to have. Any physical object is either spherical or not; no nonphysical object could be spherical. Therefore the term "spherical" is either applicable or nonapplicable to any particular or indeed to anything whatever.

This use of the term "character" allows us to restrict the term "characteristic" to characters that things actually have, whereas use of the term "character" does not imply either that something has it or that nothing does. Thus I can speak of the character a coin in my pocket may have of being dated "1952," without it following either that a coin of that date is there or is not. Again, undoubtedly there exist many things with many characteristics that have neither been noticed nor even conceived. These are characters that are actually embodied or possessed or exemplified by particulars even though they have not been either noticed or thought of. They belong to the genus, character, and to the species, characteristic, that is, characters that as a matter of fact characterize. But the realization that there are characters—which are also characteristics—that have never been conceived makes us want to distinguish between characters that have been conceived and characters that have not been. We can call conceived characters "concepts." But it also occurs to us that there may be some characters that are at a given time neither conceived nor exemplified. Let us call them, for want of a better name, "pure characters." Of course we can not mention any of these for we haven't yet conceived them, nor can we point to particulars that exemplify them. But it seems highly likely, for instance, that out of the infinity of positive integers there must be many that are neither instanced nor conceived. In summary, then, a *characteristic* is an embodied character, a *concept* is a conceived character, a *pure character* is a character that is neither embodied nor conceived. There are thus three species of the genus character.

One advantage of introducing this terminology is that it enables us to distinguish and state succinctly the various positions that have been traditionally discussed under the name "the problem of universals."

(B) *What major kinds of characters are there?* (1) *Nominalism:* This is the view that there are no characters of any kind, neither characteristics nor concepts nor pure characters. Perhaps one consideration that has led some very able philosophers to be nominalists is that characters are not perceptible or manipulable as physical objects are. Since they are not discoverable in perception, considerations of economy might suggest avoiding the supposition that such entities exist. (See the Quine selection.)

This view is shown to be false if characters of any of these kinds exist. The argument here is directed to show that there are characteristics. There is a strong *prima facie* case for them. We ordinarily agree without question, for example, that this desk and that one both have tops which are flat and rectangular. They differ in other respects, but both embody the characters mentioned. Hence there exist at least three characteristics. Or, again, here are two different books, but both are alike in being books and in containing precisely 216 pages. Being a book and containing precisely 216 pages are characteristics common to both books. Extreme nominalists are forced to deny this together with all common qualities, properties, and relations.

The denial of characteristics has led extreme nominalists, like E. B. McGilvary, A. Korzybski, and S. I. Hayakawa,[10] to deny that particulars are alike in any respect. According to this type of view it would be a mistake to think, for example, of all cows as having certain bovine qualities. Instead, we should speak of cow_1 and cow_2 and cow_3 and so on. Why do we call them all cows? Nominalists of this sort cannot of course answer: "because of common characteristics"; they try instead to say that all cows are similar, though not alike in any respect. But, of course, as Russell and others have pointed out, we can then ask the same kind of question about relations of similarity, and the thoroughgoing nominalist must deny also that these are alike in any respect. We have only $similarity_1$ holding between cow_1 and cow_2, say, and $similarity_2$ holding say between cow_2 and cow_3. But according to this kind of nominalism these two relations of similarity have nothing in common. They are at most similiar in another sense, that of $similarity_3$. This type of view avoids commitment to an infinity of characteristics only by accepting commitment to an infinity of distinct relations of similarity. And it makes for epistemological problems, that is, problems in the theory of knowledge, of extreme difficulty, with no satisfactory answers forthcoming, as to how we can recognize and distinguish a new relation of similarity holding between any two relations of similarity already picked out. In what respects, we can ask, do these three relations differ? Another way of noting the basic difficulty of such a complete denial of abstract entities, that is, nonparticulars, is to call attention to the fact that an extreme nominalist of this kind must get along with a vocabulary consisting only of proper names. But no series of proper names can convey descriptive information about the items named.

W. V. Quine (p. 78) has long admitted that many predicate terms, for example, "square," which seem to refer to characteristics, are indeed meaningful and apply correctly to a number of particu-

[10] Cf. Bibliography at end of this book.

lars. But he has wanted to deny that they refer to meanings of which certain assertions are true. Rather, he has advocated trying to construct a language that does not allow terms of this sort or their cognate subject terms, for example, "squareness" to designate or name anything. But he does admit that we often want to say such things as that implication is transitive, or that combustibility is a function of various component factors. For a long time he hoped to avoid by contextual definitions the use of such terms as subjects. But he admits in *Word and Object* [11] that he has now abandoned this project and along with it his nominalism. He now admits certain abstract entities, namely classes, for without them, he has concluded, mathematics would be much too poor. C. D. Broad once defined "a silly view" as one that only a very able philosopher would ever try to defend. Quine tried for many years to be a nominalist but has now given up.

(2) *Conceptualism:* On the positive side this is the view that we can and do conceive characters. There are concepts. On the negative side, conceptualists deny both characteristics and pure characters. The arguments against nominalism tend to show that there are characteristics, and those against extreme realism,[12] below, attempt to prove that there are pure characters. In their denials of characteristics and pure characters conceptualists seem to be mistaken. That they are correct in their positive assertion that there are concepts, however, seems to be shown by consideration of the attempts of Berkeley and Hume to prove that there could not possibly be any concepts, or abstract ideas, as they called them.

They argued that it is impossible to imagine any abstract idea, for example, a triangle in general, one that would be representative of no one species of triangle nor any individual triangle, but yet would be an image of any triangle of any kind. Abstract images, they concluded, are manifestly impossible, and hence so are abstract ideas. But this line of argument, followed by both Berkeley and Hume, loses its force as soon as we distinguish between imagining

[11] Cambridge: The Technology Press of Massachusetts Institute of Technology, 1960, p. 267.

[12] The realism considered throughout this section is a very different theory from the realistic theory about particulars or substances considered in Part I. Here what is maintained is the reality or existence of characters. Conceptualists admit the existence of concepts, moderate realists the existence of characteristics and concepts, and extreme realists the existence of pure characters, of concepts, and of characteristics, that is, the existence of characters of any of these three types.

and conceiving. It is indeed impossible to imagine an abstract image, but it seems not at all impossible to conceive an abstract idea. "To conceive" is not equivalent to "to imagine abstractly" but rather to "to know the meaning of." And we do know what the term "triangle," for instance, means when used, for example in the context of plane Euclidean geometry. It signifies a plane figure bounded by three straight lines and refers to all the figures that there are of this kind.

Berkeley and Hume themselves came close to admitting the possibility of conceiving "abstract ideas," that is, concepts. Berkeley, in trying to answer the question how by imagining a particular triangle Euclid, or anyone else, could prove a general proposition in geometry, said that this is possible by imagining a particular triangle but neglecting those respects in which it differs from other particular triangles or images of them. But precisely this process of considering only the respects in which triangles are alike and neglecting those in which they differ is a form of abstraction by means of which we can arrive at an abstract idea of a triangle. Hume called attention to what we can do in considering two circles, one red and one blue, and in the same visual field, two squares, one red and one blue. By "a distinction of reason," he said, we can notice that the circles are alike in respect of shape though different in color, and similarly the squares; and also, by such a distinction we can note that the two red figures are alike in respect of color though different in respect of shape, and similarly for the two blue figures. But making such a distinction of reason is precisely what other people have called the process of attending to only certain features of an object before us and abstracting from or neglecting its other features. This is at least one way to conceive an abstract idea.

(3) *Moderate (Aristotelian) Realism:* Aristotle would have agreed that there are characteristics, that is, characters embodied in things, and also that we can and do conceive concepts. The one alternative that he and other moderate realists deny is the existence of pure characters, or, as he would have called them, "pure forms." [13]

(4) *Extreme (Platonic) Realism:* By contrast with Aristotle, Plato admitted, and indeed insisted on, the existence of many pure forms, that is pure characters. His view, and modernized forms of it, have been called "extreme realism." It is the view that there exist

---

[13] He did regard God as pure form, but that is a complication of his view which we can here neglect.

characteristics, concepts, and pure characters. The principal type of argument that favors this position takes this form:

One is to note that our number system provides an infinite number of positive integers. Since the number is infinite, it is not the case that each and every one of them has been thought of by the finite number of creatures there have been who have possessed powers of conception in the finite period since there have been such creatures. Similarly, if Einstein is right, our universe is finite and contains only a finite number of particles. Therefore there are not in existence an infinite number of material things. There could conceivably be an infinite number of spiritual beings, but there seems to be no reason why this should be so. Hence it is quite plausible to believe that certain positive numbers included in our system have never been exemplified. But if so, then it would be true also that there are such numbers which have neither been exemplified nor conceived. These would be pure characters.

7. *Facts and Propositions.* (A) Must we admit that there are facts? We have seen good reasons for admitting the existence of individuals (particulars) and characters (universals). Are these not sufficient to make any elementary statement or judgment we wish to make? Can we not tell you with their aid, for example, that Jenny is beautiful? Are we in saying this committing ourselves to more than particulars and universals? Yes, we are. For no array or list of individuals and characters tells us anything about which individuals have what characteristics. But we asserted that Jenny is beautiful, that beauty characterizes her. Only if it is a fact that Jenny is beautiful is what we said true. If there were no facts, there could be no true empirical statements.

(B) *Must we admit that there are propositions?* Let us suppose that what we asserted is not true, that there is no such fact as Jenny's being beautiful. In this case what we asserted, though we believed it to be a fact, was not a fact. What was it then that we believed and asserted? What we have done is two things: (1) call attention to a proposition, to a possible state of affairs to the effect that Jenny is beautiful, and (2) assert this proposition. If our belief in it is true, then this state of affairs is actual or factual. If it is not, we have at least led you to entertain and consider the proposition we erroneously asserted. We believed this proposition and asserted it. You, perhaps, knew that very proposition to be false and denied it.

What sort of an entity is a proposition? It is like a concept in that we can think of it or conceive it. But a proposition differs from a concept in that it is the kind of conceivable entity toward which an attitude of belief, disbelief, or doubt is appropriate. That is, we can believe a proposition, or disbelieve it, or maintain an attitude of neutral nonbelief toward it, neither believing nor disbelieving it. I can call your attention to the proposition I am entertaining and then you can entertain it, become aware of it, even if you had not thought of it before. Now you can adopt some epistemic attitude toward it, perhaps one quite different from mine. Whose attitude is correct is determined by whether there exists a fact in virtue of which the proposition is true. In asserting a proposition, we implicitly declare it to be true. But only if what we assert to be the case is in fact the case is our assertion correct and the proposition asserted true.

The relation between a proposition and the corresponding fact is somewhat like that which holds between a concept and the corresponding characteristic. Only if the character conceived is actually embodied or instantiated is there such a characteristic. Only if the proposition or state of affairs conceived is present in the world is there a corresponding fact.

Some philosophers, for example, W. V. Quine, have tried to get along with sentences and avoid accepting the notion of a meaning or proposition which the sentence, if it is meaningful, conveys. But they run into very serious difficulties, especially in the translation of sentences in indirect discourse, in trying to determine when two sentences are equivalent without determining whether they have the same meaning. A good question for students to consider is this: Would not the reasons that justified Quine in giving up nominalism and accepting classes (and by implication, the concepts determining those classes) be relevant and strong reasons for accepting propositions?

III. THE NATURE OF METAPHYSICS

The sample of typical metaphysical problems and procedures we have now examined, though far from exhaustive, does nevertheless provide a reasonable basis for some modest generalizations regarding the nature of metaphysical problems and the methods used to reach metaphysical conclusions. Theorizing about these matters has sometimes been called "metametaphysics," or the philosophy of metaphysics. It raises questions not within metaphysics but about metaphysics. Although there are many questions of this kind, we limit ourselves to examining three.

8. *Metaphysical Meaningfulness:* Are metaphysical utterances meaningful?

Recently a number of philosophers, calling themselves "logical empiricists" [14] have explicitly put forward the view that metaphysical utterances are necessarily "meaningless" and could not possibly be either true or false, let alone be known as one or the other. In essence their objection stems from Kant's distinctions between analytic and synthetic judgments on the one hand and a priori and empirical judgments on the other (see Kant selection). A statement (or judgment) is a priori if it is either logically necessary or strictly universal—for example, "All even numbers have 2 as a prime factor" —otherwise it is empirical (a posteriori). A subject-predicate statement is analytic if the subject expression entails the predicate expression—for example, "All blue things are colored"—otherwise it is synthetic. All statements that are both analytic and a priori are necessarily true because of the entailment of the predicate by the subject, for example, "A brother is a male sibling." All true statements that are synthetic and empirical can be known to be true only through experience because they convey information not entailed by the subject term. For example, "It is raining here now" and "All grasses are green in color." Kant offers no examples of statements that are both analytic and empirical, because analytic statements are necessarily true and therefore a priori. He does assert, however, that there are statements that are both synthetic and a priori. We need not here examine his complex arguments but can turn instead to the arguments of logical positivists who deny that this is even possible and claim to demonstrate that every statement known to be true is either analytic or empirical.

Logical positivists ask about propositions, that is, what is asserted by a statement, how we can know which are true. An analytic a priori proposition, they agree, is known to be not merely true but necessarily true because the subject term entails the predicate term. "A red house is red" and "All points on the circumference of a circle are equidistant from the center of that circle" are typical examples. In the first case the predicate is explicitly contained in the subject; in the second, the definition of "circumference of a circle" entails "that all points on the circumference are equidistant from the center." Such analytic statements are often called "tautologies"; they

[14] Cf. Rudolf Carnap, "Philosophy and Logical Syntax," in Henry W. Johnstone, Jr., *What Is Philosophy?* (New York: The Macmillan Co., 1965), pp. 46–56.

are true, not just accidentally of this world, but hold necessarily of any possible world. They hold in virtue of the laws of logic, which are themselves tautologous in character.

By contrast, empirical propositions can be known to be true or probably true only by means of observation, measurement, and other empirical devices. Thus "The Empire State building is taller than the Chrysler building" is known to be true because the top of the former has been ascertained to be a certain number of feet farther above ground level than the latter. Again, on the basis of observation statements about the color of lawns in certain observed parts of Canada, one can generalize with probability to the conclusion that all lawns in Canada are of that color.

But if a follower of Kant advances a statement he claims is both a priori and synthetic, one asks in vain, the logical positivist claims, for evidence of its truth. Since the statement is synthetic, it cannot be a tautology. And since it is a priori, no observation can show it to be necessarily true of all possible worlds. To one who claims that he knows it is true by intuition, or because it is self-evident, it is embarrassing to be asked on what grounds he can decide between the rival claims of conflicting synthetic a priori judgments. How can one decide between a genuine intuition and a pseudo one?

A nontautologous statement, logical positivists assert, can be known to be true, if at all, by relevant observations which serve to confirm or disconfirm it. Many go farther and say that a synthetic statement is "meaningless" unless it is verifiable or falsifiable, that is, unless true observation statements render it probable or improbable. This dictum is often taken to mean that actual verification or falsification must occur before a synthetic statement is meaningful. On this interpretation, the statement, "There is granite somewhere in a certain galaxy thousands of light years away from this earth," would be meaningless for no relevant observations of that area have ever been made. For on this interpretation of the theory the statement is not meaningful if it has never been verified. Other logical positivists have suggested relaxing the term "verifiability" so that a statement may correctly be called verifiable, and hence meaningful, if it is possible to verify it, even though such verification has not yet occurred. But this modification leads to further questions. What is required to justify our saying that a statement is possible of verification even though it has not yet been verified? Must some definite verifying procedure be known that could possibly be carried out? And what is meant by "possibly," "logically possible," or "factually possible"?

C. I. Lewis (p. 99) has criticized this type of logical positivism by proposing that all that is required for a synthetic statement to be meaningful for a given reader is that he be able to envisage in imagination what sort of an experience would serve to confirm or disconfirm the statement. With the gradual shift to something like Lewis' form of the verifiability principle, most of the metaphysical statements so cavalierly dismissed have been readmitted for philosophical consideration.

9. *Metaphysical Knowledge:* Are all metaphysical problems of one type?

The problems considered in Part I of this book all raise fundamental questions about the particulars or individuals to be found in the universe. We considered the alternative views that every thing is material in nature (materialism), that everything is mental (idealism), and that there are two distinct substances in the world, mind and matter (realism). We considered also the basic question raised by absolute idealists as to whether the universe as a whole is a loosely knit structure, with many relations purely external to the things they relate, or whether it is rather like a supraorganic whole in which all relations are internal, and no change can occur anywhere without changing everything about everything. The answers favored here were to the effect that matter and mind are distinct substances, and that though any change in anything makes some change in everything, no change has the total effect envisaged by absolute idealists.

The problems considered in Part II, by contrast, were all about basic characters that can or might characterize large numbers of particulars. We considered the nature of the concept of substance and its relation to the polar concept of the characters that substances might conceivably have. We went farther and examined carefully the four most widely known theories about the nature of characters. These are all problems about universals rather than particulars, and indeed about basic categories. Part II consists thus of what is not infrequently called "categorial analysis."

10. *Metaphysical Method:* Is metaphysical method a priori or empirical?

The method of Part II, dealing with problems of categorial analysis is primarily a priori and analytic. Having ascertained which characters are most fundamental, the metaphysicians try to work out their a priori interrelationships. Which categories entail which others? Which categories are incompatible with which others? A careful scrutiny of this a priori sort is indispensable to working out a consistent and comprehensive, and preferably independent, set of basic categories. This type of method is deductive, and its goal is a deductive system, in which all concepts are entailed by a basic few, and in which all propositions are derivable from an initial set taken as primitive. This deductive, a priori type of procedure for discovering the basic categories and studying their logical relations represents one of the classical methods recurrent throughout the history of philosophy, that of the great rationalists, for example, Plato, Spinoza, and Leibniz.

In order to try to answer satisfactorily the questions raised in Part I, on the other hand, it is necessary to turn to observation and generalization, to the inductive procedures characteristic of the empirical sciences. How could we know whether there are particulars that are material without observing at least one? How could we know that there are particulars that are mental unless we are acquainted with at least one? How were we justified in deciding to favor realism over both idealism and materialism save by examining minds and material things and finding that the characteristics of neither can be accounted for in terms of the characteristics of the other? And how could we reject the view that all relations are internal save by finding some that are external, and noting that though a change in such a relation changes some of the things about the relata it does not change everything about them?

In short the study of metaphysics undertaken in this book seems to indicate that there are two quite different subject-matter fields and there are two quite different methods used in typical metaphysical treatises by famous philosophers. The method used for answering questions about particulars is primarily empirical; the method used for answering questions about universals is primarily rationalistic, that is, a priori. To be sure, deductive reasoning is useful in extending our knowledge of particulars, and observation is useful for checking the applicability of concepts attained by a priori methods. But on balance, there seems to be substantially more empirical knowledge used in developing philosophical ideas about particulars, substantially more a priori knowledge used in developing a system of categories.

There are, of course, some philosophers who have been almost wholly rationalistic in method and have been concerned almost entirely with problems of categorial analysis. Kant is a prime example, Spinoza another. But there have been other philosophers who have been fundamentally empirical in their methods, and who have taken as their starting point in their philosophical work the observational data about particulars they and others have amassed through experience, for example, Berkeley and Hume. One can indeed lay down rules arbitrarily and say that he will regard nothing as metaphysics unless it is knowledge of the relations of basic categories, knowledge gained by the rationalistic deductive method. Or one can equally arbitrarily lay down the principle that he will call nothing metaphysics unless it is knowledge of particulars of very general kinds, knowledge resting on observation and induction, on empirical rather than rationalistic methods. But if we are trying to reach a conclusion based on what great philosophers over the ages have actually done when they were philosophizing, we would fall into error by ruling out either the subject matter or the methods of so large and eminent a group of them as either the rationalists or the empiricists. The conclusion suggested is that metaphysics includes both types of subject matter and both types of knowledge-seeking procedures.

PART I

Metaphysical Doctrines and Schools

HUGH ELLIOT

Materialism

Hugh Elliot (1881–1930), educated at Trinity College, Cambridge, became a writer, rather than a teacher. He published books on Spencer and Bergson, edited the letters of J. S. Mill, and wrote on Human Character. *Always interested in science, he published in 1919 the book from which this selection is taken. He asserts the extreme materialistic position that "the mind is the sum total of cerebral conditions."*

I am now about to deny altogether the existence of any physical entity to be called mind, apart from the neural processes which are supposed to accompany the workings of that entity. I am about to argue that the only possible meaning to be given to the name "mind" is the sum-total of those material neural processes, and that they are not accompanied by a shadowy entity, meaningless and powerless, as assumed in current physiological discussions.

We reached the conclusion in a previous chapter that the bodily organism is a complex machine. We found that all its processes and activities are attributable to physicochemical forces, identical with those which are recognized in the inorganic realm. We learnt that there is no "vital force" or other spiritual interference with the normal physical sequences. If, then, there be a mind, it is reduced to the function of inertly and uselessly accompanying the activities of certain neural elements. This is the doctrine of epiphenomenalism, and it is the last word possible to one who accepts the duality of mind and matter. It is a theory which on the face of it is devoid of

From Hugh Elliot, *Modern Science and Materialism* (London: Longmans, Green & Co. Ltd., 1919), pp. 191–197. Used by permission of Longmans, Green.

verisimilitude. What can be the use of such a shadowy and inefficient entity? What parallel can be found in Nature for the existence of so gratuitous a superfluity? Moreover, what mechanism, conceivable or inconceivable, could cause it thus to shadow neural processes, which *ex hypothesi* do not produce it? If one such mental state is the cause of the next, how does it happen that it causes the one which is necessary to accompany the actual neural process at the moment? Epiphenomenalism involves us in a pre-established harmony that is profoundly opposed to the scientific spirit of the twentieth century. The problem, however, is not one that need be discussed on the grounds of *a priori* probability. It is a theory that may be rigidly refuted, and to that task I now turn.

It is a part of the doctrine of epiphenomenalism that a man would to all external appearance be precisely the same whether he was possessed of his epiphenomenal mind or not. Conduct, action, expression, would not in the slightest extent be affected were he completely devoid of mind and consciousness; for all these things depend upon material sequences alone. Men are puppets or automata, and we have no further grounds for supposing them to have minds than the fact that we know we have a mind ourselves, and the argument by analogy from ourselves to them. But arguments from analogy are notoriously insecure, and it seems, therefore, to be quite within the bounds of possibility to the epiphenomenalist that some or all other men may be mindless syntheses of matter. Descartes did, indeed, affirm this very thing of lower animals.

Now let us assume that such a man actually exists, or, if you prefer, let us assume that physical chemistry has advanced to such a pitch that a man may be synthetized in the laboratory, starting from the elements, carbon, nitrogen, etc., of which protoplasm is composed. Let us assume in any case a "synthetic man" without a mind, yet indistinguishable by the epiphenomenalist hypothesis from another man identically constituted materially but having a mind. Ask the synthetic man whether he has a mind. What will he say? Inevitably he will say yes. For he must say the same thing as the man, identically made, who *has* a mind. Otherwise the same question would set up different responses in the nervous systems of the two, and that is by hypothesis impossible. The sound of the words "have you a mind?" entering the ears of the synthetic man sets up highly complex cerebral associations (which we call grasping their meaning); these associations will, after a short time, culminate in nervous currents to the tongue, lips and larynx, which will be moved in such a way as to produce an audible and intelligent answer. Now this answer must be the same in the case of the man who has a mind as in the case of the mindless man, since their nervous systems are the same. If there was a different vocal response to an identical aural stimulus, then there must in one of them have been some external interference with the physico-chemical sequences. Mind must have broken through the chain of physical causality, and that is contrary to hypothesis.

What can the epiphenomenalist say? That the mindless man is a liar, to say he has a mind? That will not do, for if the two men are objectively identical one cannot be a liar, and the other not; one engaged in deceit, while the other speaks the truth. The epiphenomenalist is thrown back, therefore, on the assumption that the mindless man has made a mistake; that he thinks he has a mind, but really has not one; that his nervous constitution is such as to impel him to the conviction that he has a mind when he really has not, to lead him to talk upon psychical phenomena and their differences from matter, and in general to behave exactly as if he knew all about mind and matter, had considered the subject of their relationship, etc.

The example shows, furthermore, that the condition of "knowing one has a mind" is a condition which can be stated and accounted for in rigidly materialistic terms. When the epiphenomenalist himself asserts that he has a mind, the movements of his vocal cords by which he makes that pronouncement are by his own theory led up to by a chain of purely material sequences. He would make just the same pronouncement if he had no mind at all. His claim to possess a mind, therefore, is wholly irrelevant to the real question whether he actually has a mind or not. The events that make him say he has a mind are not the actual possession of a mind, but those cerebral processes which, in epiphenomenalist language, are said to underlie states of consciousness. It is the cerebral processes alone which make him speak, and his utterance, his belief in a mind, furnish testimony alone to the existence of those cerebral processes. Were the mind truly able to compel a belief and an announcement of its own existence, it could only be by breaking through the chain of material bodily sequences, and this is a vitalistic supposition that is ruled out by physiology. The belief in the possession of a mind is a cerebral condition, due, not to the actual possession of a mind, but to definite pre-existing cerebral conditions on the same material plane.

I do not see how epiphenomenalism could be much more

effectively refuted. Yet it is the only respectable dualistic theory that is compatible with physiological mechanism. Let me recapitulate for a moment the facts, now before us, upon which we have to establish a theory of the relationship of mind and body.

Physiology has shown that bodily activity of every kind is a product of purely material sequences, into the course of which there is no irruption of any spiritualistic factor. On the dualistic theory, that doctrine is excessively difficult to understand. You move your arm by an act of will, or what seems to be a non-material cause, and yet it is conclusively established that the movement of the arm is due to definite material changes occurring in the brain, and caused by the fixed laws of physics and chemistry in the most determinist fashion. Now, anchoring ourselves firmly to that fact, we are confronted with the problem of where to put the mind. For every mental state there is some corresponding cerebral state; the one appears to be the exact counterpart of the other down to the smallest discoverable particular. Now on the dualistic assumption, there is only one possible hypothesis, namely, that of epiphenomenalism. Or, rather, it is incorrect to call it an hypothesis; for *if* there are two things, mind and body, epiphenomenalism is no more than a statement of the facts established by physiology and psychology. Dualistic physiologists, therefore, are practically forced to accept it. Yet, as I have shown, it is utterly untenable when properly thought out.

We are faced, therefore, by two possible alternatives: (1) to abandon mechanism, (2) to abandon dualism. Now mechanism is a physiological theory which is proved. We must hold fast to it therefore at any expense to our metaphysical preconceptions. The only remaining alternative, then, is the abandonment of dualism. We must affirm that there is no thin shadow accompanying cerebral processes as alleged; that there are *not* two things, mind and body, fundamentally distinct. We must, in short, affirm that the mind *is* the cerebral processes themselves, not an imaginary accompaniment of them; and this, it will be noticed, is precisely the conclusion at which we arrived by different arguments in an earlier part of the present chapter. When we recollect that matter is but one form of experience, while mental manifestations are another similar form; when we recollect that elementary experiences may be associated into larger groups, we shall scarcely have greater difficulty in understanding how a sensation can be identified with a cerebral process than we have in understanding how, for instance, redness and hardness can be identified as properties of one material object.

I have said that mind is not an independent existence, but that it is a name for the sum-total of certain kinds of nervous or cerebral processes, and that it is therefore to be identified with phenomena of a material order. The difficulty of grasping this proposition will be very largely mitigated by the fact that there exists a phenomenon from the inorganic world which furnishes a remarkably true and precise analogy to this strange product of the organic world. The phenomenon to which I refer is the phenomenon of fire. In very early Greek philosophy, the Universe was believed to consist of earth, air, fire, and water. Fire was held to be a distinct entity on a par with the other three. We now know that it is not itself an entity of any kind, but is a manifestation of a certain chemical process, as for instance, the oxidation of carbon, in the course of which the carbon particles give forth light and heat. There is nothing whatever present in a flame except these molecules undergoing chemical change; yet, to an uneducated eye, the flame seems to be a distinct entity, differing altogether from a mere collection of chemically active material particles.

We may interpret the existence of mind in a precisely analogous manner. All that really exists is the material particles of the substance of the nervous system. When these particles enter upon a certain kind of chemical activity, the effect is to suggest the existence of some new kind of elusive non-material entity called mind. But this entity has no more real existence than has fire. In each case we have to do exclusively with molecules undergoing disintegration or combination. This chemical activity suffices in itself to account for the whole of the phenomena flowing from the centre of activity, and the belief in any additional independent entity is a fallacy which itself can be expressed and explained in physico-chemical terms. The flames of a fire flash out swiftly in all directions and vanish again, to reappear instantly in a closely similar form. So, too, the ideation or emotion of the individual may open up new avenues of mind for a brief moment, as they travel on to a new position. In each case the fluctuations of form are due to the constantly changing area of chemical activity; and just as the fire maintains for short periods a relative constancy of size and shape, so the mental content of an individual is apt to remain for a time at about the same value of intensity, and fastened to the same subjects of attention. At times the fire burns low; at other times it bursts forth into exuberant activity. The accuracy of the analogy is due to the fact that both phenomena are based upon the same foundation; the one is a manifestation from inorganic matter, while the other is a manifestation from organic matter, and therefore immeasurably more complex as to its chemistry.

When once we have got over the shock which monism carries to those accustomed to think in dualistic terms, we find that the great majority of the difficulties of metaphysics fall away. By an act of will I raise my arm. The plain man insists that his will did it; the physiologist knows that it was physico-chemical processes in the brain. The dilemma is at once overcome when the philosopher points out that the will *is* the physico-chemical processes, and that they both mean the same thing. The whole controversy of free-will and determinism is resolved by the discovery that each side means exactly the same thing, the only difference being in the terms used. The difficulty of the epiphenomenalist is also solved. He says he has a mind. What makes him say so is not a transcendental "knowledge of having mind," but a certain cerebral state. When we have affirmed the absolute identity of that knowledge with that cerebral state, all difficulties vanish. The mind is the sum-total of cerebral conditions. He says he has a mind; it is the existence of the cerebral conditions which cause him to say so. He says he has a mind because he has cerebral conditions, and his remark is true and intelligible only on the one hypothesis that the mind *is* the cerebral conditions.

Idealism

George Berkeley (1685–1753), Fellow of Trinity College, Dublin at twenty-two, Bishop of Cloyne at forty-nine, published A New Theory of Vision *in 1709,* The Principles of Human Knowledge *in 1710, and* Three Dialogues between Hylas and Philonous *in 1713. He spent the years 1728–31 in Rhode Island. Creator and subtle defender of subjective idealism, he has profoundly influenced modern idealistic philosophy.*

It is evident to any one who takes a survey of the *objects* of human knowledge, that they are either ideas actually imprinted on the senses; or else such as are perceived by attending to the passions and operations of the mind; or lastly, ideas formed by help of memory and imagination—either compounding, dividing, or barely representing those originally perceived in the aforesaid ways. By sight I have the ideas of light and colours, with their several degrees and variations. By touch I perceive hard and soft, heat and cold, motion and resistance, and of all these more and less either as to quantity or degree. Smelling furnishes me with odours; the palate with tastes; and hearing conveys sounds to the mind in all their variety of tone and composition. And as several of these are observed to accompany each other, they come to be marked by one name, and so to be reputed as one thing. Thus, for example, a certain colour, taste, smell, figure and consistence having been observed to go together, are accounted one distinct thing, signified by the name *apple;* other collections of ideas constitute a stone, a tree, a book, and the like sensible things—which as they are pleasing or disagreeable excite the passions of love, hatred, joy, grief, and so forth.

2.

But, besides all that endless variety of ideas or objects of knowledge, there is likewise something which knows or perceives them, and exercises divers operations, as willing, imagining, remembering, about them. This perceiving, active being is what I call *mind, spirit, soul,* or *myself.* By which words I do not denote any one of my ideas, but a thing entirely distinct from them, wherein, they exist,

From George Berkeley, *The Principles of Human Knowledge* (La Salle, Ill.: Open Court Publishing Co., 1910), secs. 1–4, 6–9, 15.

or, which is the same thing, whereby they are perceived—for the existence of an idea consists in being perceived.

3.

That neither our thoughts, nor passions, nor ideas formed by the imagination, exist without the mind, is what everybody will allow. And it seems no less evident that the various sensations or ideas imprinted on the sense, however blended or combined together (that is, whatever objects they compose), cannot exist otherwise than in a mind perceiving them.—I think an intuitive knowledge may be obtained of this by any one that shall attend to what is meant by the term *exists*, when applied to sensible things. The table I write on I say exists, that is, I see and feel it; and if I were out of my study I should say it existed—meaning thereby that if I was in my study I might perceive it, or that some other spirit actually does perceive it. There was an odour, that is, it was smelt; there was a sound, that is, it was heard; a colour or figure, and it was perceived by sight or touch. This is all that I can understand by these and the like expressions. For as to what is said of the absolute existence of unthinking things without any relation to their being perceived, that seems perfectly unintelligible. Their *esse* is *percipi*, nor is it possible they should have any existence out of the minds or thinking things which perceive them.

4.

It is indeed an opinion strangely prevailing amongst men, that houses, mountains, rivers, and in a word all sensible objects, have an existence, natural or real, distinct from their being perceived by the understanding. But, with how great an assurance and acquiescence soever this principle may be entertained in the world, yet whoever shall find it in his heart to call it in question may, if I mistake not, perceive it to involve a manifest contradiction. For, what are the fore-mentioned objects but the things we perceive by sense? and what do we perceive besides our own ideas or sensations? and is it not plainly repugnant that any one of these, or any combination of them, should exist unperceived?

6.

Some truths there are so near and obvious to the mind that a man need only open his eyes to see them. Such I take this important one to be, viz., that all the choir of heaven and furniture of the earth, in a word all those bodies which compose the mighty frame of the world, have not any subsistence without a mind, that their *being* is to be perceived or known; that consequently so long as they are not actually perceived by me, or do not exist in my mind or that of any other created spirit, they must either have no existence at all, or else subsist in the mind of some Eternal Spirit—it being perfectly unintelligible, and involving all the absurdity of abstraction, to attribute to any single part of them an existence independent of a spirit. [To be convinced of which, the reader need only reflect, and try to separate in his own thoughts the *being* of a sensible thing from its *being perceived.*]

7.

From what has been said it follows there is not any other Substance than *Spirit,* or that which perceives. But, for the fuller proof of this point, let it be considered the sensible qualities are colour, figure, motion, smell, taste, etc., *i. e.* the ideas perceived by sense. Now, for an idea to exist in an unperceiving thing is a manifest contradiction, for to have an idea is all one as to perceive; that therefore wherein colour, figure, and the like qualities exist must perceive them; hence it is clear there can be no unthinking substance or *substratum* of those ideas.

8.

But, say you, though the ideas themselves do not exist without the mind, yet there may be things like them, whereof they are copies or resemblances, which things exist without the mind in an unthinking substance. I answer, an idea can be like nothing but an idea; a colour or figure can be like nothing but another colour or figure. If we look but never so little into our thoughts, we shall find it impossible for us to conceive a likeness except only between our ideas. Again, I ask whether those supposed originals or external things, of which our ideas are the pictures or representations, be themselves perceivable or no? If they are, then they are ideas and we have gained our point; but if you say they are not, I appeal to any one whether it be sense to assert a colour is like something which is invisible; hard or soft, like something which is intangible; and so of the rest.

9.

Some there are who make a distinction betwixt *primary* and *secondary* qualities. By the former they mean extension, figure, motion, rest, solidity or impenetrability, and number; by the latter they denote all other sensible qualities, as colours, sounds, tastes, and so forth. The ideas we have of these they acknowledge not to be the resemblances of anything existing without the mind, or unperceived, but they will have our ideas of the primary qualities to be patterns or images of things which exist without the mind, in an unthinking substance which they call Matter. By Matter, therefore, we are to understand an inert, senseless substance, in which extension, figure, and motion do actually subsist. But it is evident from what we have already shown, that extension, figure, and motion are only ideas existing in the mind, and that an idea can be like nothing but another idea, and that consequently neither they nor their archetypes can exist in an unperceiving substance. Hence, it is plain that the very notion of what is called *Matter* or *corporeal substance*, involves a contradiction in it.

15.

In short, let any one consider those arguments which are thought manifestly to prove that colours and taste exist only in the mind, and he shall find they may with equal force be brought to prove the same thing of extension, figure, and motion. Though it must be confessed this method of arguing does not so much prove that there is no extension or colour in an outward object, as that we do not know by sense which is the true extension or colour of the object. But the arguments foregoing plainly show it to be impossible that any colour or extension at all, or other sensible quality whatsoever, should exist in an unthinking subject without the mind, or in truth, that there should be any such thing as an outward object.

BERTRAND RUSSELL

Presentational Realism

Bertrand Russell (1872–   ), Fellow of Trinity College, Cambridge, and a Nobel Prize winner, is more widely known than any other contemporary philosopher. He has published extensively and made notable contributions in many fields of philosophy: logic, epistemology, metaphysics, social philosophy, philosophy of mathematics and philosophy of science. In the early edition of Our Knowledge of the External World, *excerpted here, he urges the provocative view that physical objects are classes of sense data.*

I think it may be laid down quite generally that, *in so far* as physics or common sense is verifiable, it must be capable of interpretation in terms of actual sense-data alone. The reason for this is simple. Verification consists always in the occurrence of an expected sense-datum. Astronomers tell us there will be an eclipse of the moon: we look at the moon, and find the earth's shadow biting into it, that is to say, we see an appearance quite different from that of the usual full moon. Now if an expected sense-datum constitutes a verification, what was asserted must have been about sense-data; or, at any rate, if part of what was asserted was not about sense-data, then only the other part has been verified. . . .

The first thing to realize is that there are no such things as "illusions of sense." Objects of sense, even when they occur in dreams, are the most indubitably real objects known to us. What, then, makes us call them unreal in dreams? Merely the unusual nature of their connection with other objects of sense. I dream that I am in America, but I wake up and find myself in England without those intervening days on the Atlantic which, alas! are inseparably connected with a "real" visit to America. Objects of sense are called "real" when they have the kind of connection with other objects of sense which experience has led us to regard as normal; when they fail in this, they are called "illusions." But what is illusory is only the inferences to which they give rise; in themselves, they are every bit as real as the objects of waking life. . . .

From Bertrand Russell, *Our Knowledge of the External World* (La Salle, Ill.: Open Court Publishing Co., 1914), pp. 1, 85–93, 108–110, *passim.* Used by permission of Open Court and of George Allen & Unwin Ltd., London.

Let us imagine that each mind looks out upon the world, as in Leibniz's monadology, from a point of view peculiar to itself; and for the sake of simplicity let us confine ourselves to the sense of sight, ignoring minds which are devoid of this sense. Each mind sees at each moment an immensely complex three-dimensional world; but there is absolutely nothing which is seen by two minds simultaneously. When we say that two people see the same thing, we always find that, owing to difference of point of view, there are differences, however slight, between their immediate sensible objects. (I am here assuming the validity of testimony, but as we are only constructing a *possible* theory, that is a legitimate assumption.) The three-dimensional world seen by one mind therefore contains no place in common with that seen by another, for places can only be constituted by the things in or around them. Hence we may suppose, in spite of the differences between the different worlds, that each exists entire exactly as it is perceived, and might be exactly as it is even if it were not perceived. We may further suppose that there are an infinite number of such worlds which are in fact unperceived. If two men are sitting in a room, two somewhat similar worlds are perceived by them; if a third man enters and sits between them, a third world, intermediate between the two previous worlds, begins to be perceived. It is true that we cannot reasonably suppose just this world to have existed before, because it is conditioned by the sense-organs, nerves, and brain of the newly arrived man; but we can reasonably suppose that *some* aspect of the universe existed from that point of view, though no one was perceiving it. The system consisting of all views of the universe perceived and unperceived, I shall call the system of "perspectives"; I shall confine the expression "private worlds" to such views of the universe as are actually perceived. Thus a "private world" is a perceived "perspective"; but there may be any number of unperceived perspectives.

Two men are sometimes found to perceive very similar perspectives, so similar that they can use the same words to describe them. They say they see the same table, because the differences between the two tables they see are slight and not practically important. Thus it is possible, sometimes, to establish a correlation by similarity between a great many of the things of one perspective, and a great many of the things of another. In case the similarity is very great, we say the points of view of the two perspectives are near together in space; but this space in which they are near together is totally different from the spaces inside the two perspectives. It is a relation between the perspectives, and is not in either of them; no one can perceive it, and if it is to be known it can be only by inference. Between two perceived perspectives which are similar, we can imagine a whole series of other perspectives, some at least unperceived, and such that between any two, however similar, there are others still more similar. In this way the space which consists of relations between perspectives can be rendered continuous, and (if we choose) three-dimensional.

We can now define the momentary common-sense "thing," as opposed to its momentary appearances. By the similarity of neighbouring perspectives, many objects in the one can be correlated with objects in the other, namely, with the similar objects. Given an object in one perspective, form the system of all the objects correlated with it in all the perspectives; that system may be identified with the momentary common-sense "thing." Thus an aspect of a "thing" is a member of the system of aspects which *is* the "thing" at that moment. (The correlation of the times of different perspectives raises certain complications, of the kind considered in the theory of relativity; but we may ignore these at present.) All the aspects of a thing are real, whereas the thing is a mere logical construction. It has, however, the merit of being neutral as between different points of view, and of being visible to more than one person, in the only sense in which it can ever be visible, namely, in the sense that each sees one of its aspects.

It will be observed that, while each perspective contains its own space, there is only one space in which the perspectives themselves are the elements. There are as many private spaces as there are perspectives; there are therefore at least as many as there are percipients, and there may be any number of others which have a merely material existence and are not seen by anyone. But there is only one perspective-space, whose elements are single perspectives, each with its own private space. We have now to explain how the private space of a single perspective is correlated with part of one all-embracing perspective space.

Perspective space is the system of "points of view" of private spaces (perspectives), or, since "points of view" have not been defined, we may say it is the system of the private spaces themselves. These private spaces will each count as one point, or at any rate as one element, in perspective space. They are ordered by means of their similarities. Suppose, for example, that we start from one which contains the appearance of a circular disc, such as would be called a penny, and suppose this appearance, in the perspective in question, is circular, not elliptic. We can then form a whole series of perspectives containing a graduated series of circular aspects of varying sizes: for this purpose we only have to move (as we say) towards the penny or away from it. The perspectives in which the penny looks circular will be said to lie on a straight line in perspective space, and their order on this line will be that of the sizes of the circular aspects. Moreover—though this statement must be noticed and subsequently examined—the perspectives in which the penny looks big will be said to be nearer to the penny than those in which it looks small. It is to be remarked also that any other "thing" than our penny might have been chosen to define the relations of our perspectives in perspective space, and that experience shows that the same spatial order of perspectives would have resulted.

In order to explain the correlation of private spaces with perspective space, we have first to explain what is meant by "the place (in perspective space) where a thing is." For this purpose, let us again consider the penny which appears in many perspectives. We formed a straight line of perspectives in which the penny looked circular, and we agreed that those in which it looked larger were to be considered as nearer to the penny. We can form another straight line of perspectives in which the penny is seen end-on and looks like a straight line of a certain thickness. These two lines will meet in a certain place in perspective space, *i. e.* in a certain perspective, which may be defined as "the place (in perspective space) where the penny is." It is true that, in order to prolong our lines until they reach this place, we shall have to make use of other things besides the penny, because, so far as experience goes, the penny ceases to present any appearance after we have come so near to it that it touches the eye. But this raises no real difficulty, because the spatial order of perspectives is found empirically to be independent of the particular "things" chosen for defining the order. We can, for example, remove our penny and prolong each of our two straight lines up to their intersection by placing other pennies further off in such a way that the aspects of the one are circular where those of our original penny were circular, the aspects of the other are straight where those of our original penny were straight. There will then be just one perspective in which one of the new pennies looks circular and the other straight. This will be, by definition, the place where the original penny was in perspective space.

The above is, of course, only a first rough sketch of the way in which our definition is to be reached. It neglects the size of the penny, and it assumes that we can remove the penny without being disturbed by any simultaneous changes in the positions of other things. But it is plain that such niceties cannot affect the principle, and can only introduce complications in its application.

Having now defined the perspective which is the place where a given thing is, we can understand what is meant by saying that the perspectives in which a thing looks large are nearer to the thing than those in which it looks small: they are, in fact, nearer to the perspective which is the place where the thing is

We can now also explain the correlation between a private space and parts of perspective space. If there is an aspect of a given thing in a certain private space, then we correlate the place where this aspect is in the private space with the place where the thing is in perspective space.

We may define "here" as the place, in perspective space, which is occupied by our private world. Thus we can now understand what is meant by speaking of a thing as near to or far from "here." A thing is near to "here" if the place where it is is near to my private world. We can also understand what is meant by saying that our private world is inside our head; for our private world is a place in perspective space, and may be part of the place where our head is.

It will be observed that *two* places in perspective space are associated with every aspect of a thing: namely, the place where the thing is, and the place which is the perspective of which the aspect in question forms part. Every aspect of a thing is a member of two different classes of aspects, namely: (1) the various aspects of the thing, of which at most one appears in any given perspective; (2) the perspective of which the given aspect is a member, *i. e.* that in which the thing has the given aspect. The physicist naturally classifies aspects in the first way, the psychologist in the second. The two places associated with a single aspect correspond to the two ways of classifying it. We may distinguish the two places as that *at* which, and that *from* which, the aspect appears. The "place at which" is the place of the thing to which the aspect belongs; the "place from which" is the place of the perspective to which the aspect belongs.

Let us now endeavour to state the fact that the aspect which a thing presents at a given place is affected by the intervening medium. The aspects of a thing in different perspectives are to be conceived as spreading outwards from the place where the thing is, and undergoing various changes as they get further away from this place. The laws according to which they change cannot be stated if we only take account of the aspects that are near the thing, but require that we should also take account of the things that are at the places from which these aspects appear. This empirical fact can, therefore, be interpreted in terms of our construction.

We have now constructed a largely hypothetical picture of the world, which contains and places the experienced facts, including those derived from testimony. The world we have constructed can, with a certain amount of trouble, be used to interpret the crude facts of sense, the facts of physics, and the facts of physiology. It is therefore a world which *may* be actual. It fits the facts, and there is no empirical evidence against it; it also is free from logical impossibilities. . . .

The problem is: by what principles shall we select certain data from the chaos, and call them all appearances of the same thing?

A rough and approximate answer to this question is not very difficult. There are certain fairly stable collections of appearances, such as landscapes, the furniture of rooms, the faces of acquaintances. In these cases, we have little hesitation in regarding them on successive occasions as appearances of one thing or collection of things. But, as the *Comedy of Errors* illustrates, we may be led astray if we judge by mere resemblance. This shows that something more is involved, for two different things may have any degree of likeness up to exact similarity.

Another insufficient criterion of one thing is *continuity*. As we have already seen, if we watch what we regard as one changing thing, we usually find its changes to be continuous so far as our senses can perceive. We are thus led to assume that, if we see two finitely different appearances at two different times, and if we have reason to regard them as belonging to the same thing, then there was a continuous series of intermediate states of that thing during the time when we were not observing it. And so it comes to be thought that continuity of change is necessary and sufficient to constitute one thing. But in fact it is neither. It is not *necessary*, because the unobserved states, in the case where our attention has not been concentrated on the thing throughout, are purely hypothetical, and cannot possibly be our ground for supposing the earlier and later appearances to belong to the same thing; on the contrary, it is because we suppose this that we assume intermediate unobserved states. Continuity is also not sufficient, since we can, for example, pass by sensibly continuous gradations from any one drop of the sea to any other drop. The utmost we can say is that discontinuity during uninterrupted observation is as a rule a mark of difference between things, though even this cannot be said in such cases as sudden explosions.

The assumption of continuity is, however, successfully made in physics. This proves something, though not anything of very obvious utility to our present problem: it proves that nothing in the known world is inconsistent with the hypothesis that all changes are really continuous, though from too great rapidity or from our lack of observation they may not always appear continuous. In this hypothetical sense, continuity may be allowed to be a *necessary* condition if two appearances are to be classed as appearances of the same thing. But it is not a *sufficient* condition, as appears from the instance of the drops in the sea. Thus something more must be sought before we can give even the roughest definition of a "thing."

What is wanted further seems to be something in the nature of fulfilment of causal laws. This statement, as it stands, is very vague, but we will endeavour to give it precision. When I speak of "causal laws," I mean any laws which connect events at different times, or even, as a limiting case, events at the same time provided the connection is not logically demonstrable. In this very general sense, the laws of dynamics are causal laws, and so are the laws correlating the simultaneous appearances of one "thing" to different senses. The question is: How do such laws help in the definition of a "thing"?

To answer this question, we must consider what it is that is proved by the empirical success of physics. What is proved is that its hypotheses, though unverifiable where they go beyond sense-data, are at no point in contradiction with sense-data, but, on the contrary, are ideally such as to render all sense-data calculable from a sufficient collection of data all belonging to a given period of time. Now physics has found it empirically possible to collect sense-data into series, each series being regarded as belonging to one "thing," and behaving, with regard to the laws of physics, in a way in which series not belonging to one thing would in general not behave. If it is to be unambiguous whether two appearances belong to the same thing or not, there must be only one way of grouping appearances so that the resulting things obey the laws of physics. It would be very difficult to prove that this is the case, but for our present purposes we may let this point pass, and assume that there is only one way. We must include in our definition of a "thing" those of its aspects, if any, which are not observed. Thus we may lay down the following definition: *Things are those series of aspects which obey the laws of physics.* That such series exist is an empirical fact, which constitutes the verifiability of physics.

Representational Realism

Arthur O. Lovejoy (1873–1962), born in Berlin, student at Paris, California, Harvard, recipient of several honorary degrees, President American Philosophical Association, 1916–17, long time Professor of Philosophy at Johns Hopkins, is especially noted for his acute critical studies and his stimulating contributions to the history of ideas. Of his many publications his Carus lectures, The Revolt Against Dualism, *are most often quoted.*

We shall . . . not initially question the supposition that there are extended external objects, such as pennies, tables, planets, and distant stars, having at least the primary and possibly also the secondary qualities; having determinable positions in a space like that of visual and tactual perception, whether or not it is identical with it; capable of motion and causal interaction; acting, by means of processes in space, upon our sense-organs; and thereby conditioning the presence in our experience of the data which, whether or not identical with the objects, are our sources of information about them. When these natural assumptions are provisionally adopted, there . . . prove to be at least five familiar aspects of experience in which it seems plain that the object of our knowing must be different in the time or place or mode of its existence, or in its character, from the perceptual or other content which is present to us at the moment when we are commonly said to be apprehending that object, and without which we should never apprehend it at all.

(1) . . . Intertemporal cognition, the knowing at one time of things which exist or events which occur at another time, seems a patent example of a mode of knowledge which we are under the necessity of regarding as potentially genuine and yet as mediate. When I remember, for example, not only is there a present awareness distinct from the past memory-object (that alone would imply only the duality of act and content), but the present awareness manifestly has, and must have, a compresent content. But the past event which we say the memory is *of* cannot be this compresent content. In saying this I am, it is true, including among the natural grounds of epistemological dualism an assumption which some dualistic philos-

From Arthur O. Lovejoy, *The Revolt Against Dualism* (La Salle, Ill.: Open Court Publishing Co., 1930), pp. 17–24, 25. Used by permission of Open Court.

ophers—and even some who repudiate the naïvely dualistic theory of memory—regard as unsound. Mr. Broad, for example, has said that there "is no general metaphysical objection to such a theory" on the ground that when an event is past it ceases to exist. "Once an event has happened it exists eternally"; past events, therefore, "are always 'there' waiting to be remembered; and there is no *a priori* reason why they should not from time to time enter unto such a relation with certain present events that they become objects of direct acquaintance." [1] This view, however, implies an inconceivable divorce of the identity of an event from its date. The things which may be said to subsist eternally are essences; and the reason why they can so subsist is that, by definition, they have no dates. They do not "exist" at all, in the sense in which dated and located things do so; and if "events" eternally existed after they had "once happened" (and when they were no longer "happening"), they would likewise exist before they happened; eternalness can hardly be an acquired character. The present image and the past event may be separate embodiments of the same essence; they are not identical particulars, because the particularity of each is undefinable apart from its temporal situation and relations. The duality of the memory-image and the bygone existence to which it refers seems to be inherent in what we *mean* by remembrance; if the two were one our intertemporal knowing would defeat its own aim of apprehending the beyond, by annulling its beyondness. The very wistfulness of memory implies such duality; the past, in being known, still inexorably keeps its distance. Plainest of all is it that a man's own experienc*ing* of yesterday, the event of his then *having* an experience, does not seem to him, in being remembered, to become to-day's experiencing. Common sense, however much inclined in its more self-confident moments to believe in direct perception, has never, I suppose, believed in direct memory; it has been well aware that what is present in retrospection is a duplicate which somehow and in some degree discloses to us the character, without constituting the existence, of its original.

(2) It is not alone in the case of memory that there is a temporal sundering, and therefore an existential duality, of the content given and the reality made known to us through that content. This second reason for dualism has not, it is true, like some of the others, always been discoverable by the simplest reflection upon every-day experience. But the fact upon which it rests has long been one of the

[1] *The Mind and its Place in Nature*, p. 252.

elementary commonplaces of physical science; and the probability of
it had suggested itself to acute minds long before its verification.
There had at times occurred to him, wrote Bacon in the *Novum
Organum*, "a very strange doubt," a *dubitatio plane monstrosa*,
"namely, whether the face of a clear and starlight sky be seen at the
instant at which it really exists, and not rather a little later; and
whether there be not, as regards our sight of heavenly bodies, a
real time and an apparent time (*tempus visum*), just as there is a
real place and an apparent place taken account of by astronomers."
For it had appeared to him "incredible that the images or rays of
the heavenly bodies could be conveyed at once to the sight through
such an immense space and did not rather take some appreciable
time in travelling to us." [2] Unfortunately for his reputation Lord
Bacon was able to overcome this doubt by invoking against it
several bad reasons, which need not be here recalled; but this subtler
medieval namesake had not only propounded but embraced and
defended the same conjecture three centuries earlier.[3] Roemer's
observation in 1675, through which it became established as one
of the fundamental theorems of empirical science, is not usually
mentioned in the histories of philosophy; but the omission merely
shows how badly the history of philosophy is commonly written,
for the discovery was as significant for epistemology as it was for
physics and astronomy. It appeared definitely to forbid that naïvely
realistic way of taking the content of visual perception to which
all men at first naturally incline. The doctrine of the finite velocity
of light meant that the sense from which most of our information
about the world beyond our epidermal surfaces is derived never
discloses anything which (in Francis Bacon's phrase) "really exists"
in that world, at the instant at which it indubitably exists in perception.[4] It is with a certain phase in the history of a distant star that
the astronomer, gazing through his telescope at a given moment,
is supposed to become acquainted; but that phase, and perhaps the
star itself, have, ages since, ceased to be; and the astronomer's
present sense-data—it has therefore seemed inevitable to say—what-

[2] *Novum Organum*, II, 46.

[3] Roger Bacon, *Opus Majus*, ed. Bridges, II, pp. 68–74.

[4] The retardation of auditory sensation must so soon and so constantly have
forced itself upon the notice of primitive man that an implicit epistemological
dualism with respect to sound may be supposed to have prevailed from an early
period in the history of the race. It was, however, a vague dualism because a
sound does not so clearly present itself as occupying a definite place, or as an
adjective of an object or event in such a place.

ever else they may be, are not identical with the realities they are believed to reveal. They might perhaps be supposed to be identical with the peripheral effect produced by the light-ray on its belated arrival at the eye—in other words, with the retinal images; but two present and inverted retinal images *here* are obviously not the same as one extinct star formerly existing elsewhere, and the duality of datum and object would therefore remain. This particular hypothesis, moreover, is excluded by the now familiar fact established by the physiological psychologists, that there is a further lag—slight, but not theoretically negligible—in the transmission of the neural impulse to the cortical center, and therefore—since the percept does not appear until the impulse reaches the brain—a difference in time between the existence of a given pair of retinal images, or any other excitation of peripheral nerve-endings, and the existence of the corresponding percept. Never, in short, if both the physiologists and the physicists are right, can the datum or character-complex presented in the perception of a given moment be regarded as anything but the report of a messenger, more or less tardy and more or less open to suspicion, from the original object which we are said to know by virtue of that perception.

(3) Another class of empirical facts which are familiar, in their simpler forms, to all men have seemed by the plainest implication to show that perceptual content, even though it appears as external to the physical organs of perception, is not identical with the particular objects about which it is supposed to convey information. It is commonly assumed that the object, or objective, of a given perception can, first of all, be identified, at least roughly, by its position in space and time. What I am "perceiving" at a certain moment is the ink-bottle two feet away from my hand, or the star a hundred light-years distant. Even if the position is defined only vaguely, the thing is at least supposed to be (or have been) "out there" somewhere. This identification of the object referred to is, obviously, possible only by means of the same perception; yet, assuming such identification, experience shows that what I perceive is determined by events or conditions intervening in space and time between that object and my so-called perception of it. The qualities sensibly presented vary with changes which appear to occur, not in the place where *the* object is supposed to exist, but in regions between it and the body itself, and, in particular, in the very organs of perception. The examples are trite: a man puts a lens before his eyes, and the size or shape or number or perceived distance of the

objects presented is altered; he puts certain drugs into his stomach, and the colors of all the perceived objects external to his body change; he swallows other drugs in sufficient quantity, and sees outside his body objects which no one else can see, and which his own other senses fail to disclose. The discovery of this primary sort of physical relativity, which is really one of the most pregnant of philosophical discoveries, begins in infancy with the earliest experience of the illusions of perspective, or the observation that the objects in the visual field change their spatial relations when looked at with first one eye and then the other. If *homo sapiens* had at the outset been blind, the first seeing man, a paleolithic Einstein, when he reported this astonishing fact—the relativity of position to the motions of eyelids—to his fellow cave-men, would presumably have seemed to them a deviser of intolerable paradoxes, and have been made acquainted with those more effective methods for repressing strange doctrines which cave-men, no doubt, knew how to employ. The evidence of this dependence of the nature of what is perceived upon happenings which, as themselves experienced, do not happen in the right place to permit them to be regarded as changes in the *cognoscendum* itself, has constantly increased with the progress of the sciences of optics, neuro-cerebral physiology, and psychology; the eventual determination of the character of the percept has been removed farther and farther, not only from the external object, but even from the external organ of sense. As Professor Dewey remarked, in the preceding series of these lectures, "it is pure fiction that a 'sensation' or peripheral excitation, or stimulus, travels undisturbed in solitary state in its own coach-and-four to either the brain or consciousness in its purity. A particular excitation is but one of an avalanche of contemporaneously occurring excitations, peripheral and from proprioceptors; each has to compete with others, to make terms with them; what happens is an integration of complex forces." [5] And even in the earliest and easiest phases of this discovery, the variability of the percept with conditions extrinsic to the object to be perceived manifestly affects those attributes by which the very identity of the individual object should be defined: it is not colors only but shapes, not shapes only but perceived positions, that prove to be functions of the processes spatially and temporally intervenient between the object and the perception, and therefore not attributable to the former. Thus what is actually perceived could be regarded only as the terminal

[5] *Experience and Nature*, first ed., p. 333.

effect of a more or less long and complex causal series of events happening at different places and times, only at the perceptually inaccessible other end of which series the *cognoscendum* was supposed to have—or rather, to have had—its being. Aside from any empirical evidences of the sort mentioned, it has apparently seemed to many minds virtually axiomatic that, if the *cognoscendum* in perception is conceived (as it is in ordinary thought and in most physical theory) as a "causal object" acting upon the bodily organs of perception in the determination of the character of the content experienced, that which is acted *upon* must also have a part—must, indeed, have the last and decisive word—in determining the character of that content. How under these circumstances the exterior causal object could be known at all is an obviously difficult question; this argument for epistemological dualism, and especially the rôle assigned in it to the organs of perception, gives rise to that "crux of realistic theories" which Mr. C. A. Strong has very precisely expressed: "to explain how a sensation which varies directly only with one physical object, the nervous system, can yet vary with another physical object sufficiently to give knowledge of it." [6] But with these ulterior difficulties we are not for the moment concerned; whatever *their* solution, they obviously do not annul the difficulty, for any realistic philosophy, of identifying the end-term with the initial term of the physico-physiological causal series.

(4) This physical and physiological conditionedness of the data manifestly implies that the contents of the experience of percipients having different spatial and physical relations to a postulated external object cannot be wholly identical. But this implication is independently confirmed and extended through that communication and comparison of experiences which is supposed to be possible through language. While the many knowers are, by the fifth article of the natural epistemological creed, dealing with what is said to be one and the same object—and if they are not doing so are not achieving what is meant by knowledge—they notoriously are not experiencing the same sensible appearances. There is an assumed identity of the region of space at which the observers are all gazing, and this serves for the requisite antecedent identification of the common *cognoscendum;* but what they severally find occupying this supposedly single locus consists of character-complexes which are not merely diverse but (according to the logic almost universally accepted until recently) contradictory. So long as it is assumed either that there are certain sets of sensible qualities—*e. g.,* two or

[6] *Mind,* N. S., 1922, p. 308.

more colors—which are incompatible, *i.e.*, cannot both occupy the same place or the same surface of a material object at the same time, or that there are in nature "things" which at a given moment have a single and harmonious outfit of geometrical and other properties, the conclusion has seemed inevitable that the many discrepant appearances cannot "really" inhabit the one place or be the one thing at that place. So soon as the dimmest notion that there is such a phenomenon as perspective distortion dawned upon men, they began *eo ipso* to be epistemological dualists. It is of course conceivable, so far as the present consideration goes, that *one* of the discordant appearances might be identical with the object-to-be-known or with some part of it; but even so, since all the other observers are also supposed to be apprehending the object, *their* apprehension, at least, must be mediated through data which are *not* identical with it. Nor does it seem a probable hypothesis that, while *almost* all perception is mediate, a few privileged observers now and then attain direct access to the object.

(5) Finally, the experience of error and illusion, however difficult it may be to render philosophically intelligible, seems to have at least one direct and obvious implication: namely, that the thing which at any moment we err about—otherwise than by mere omission—cannot be a thing which is immediately present to us at that moment, since about the latter there can be no error. It, at least, *is* what it is experienced as. In so far as *cognoscendum* and content are identified, error is excluded; in so far as the possibility of error is admitted, *cognoscendum* and content are set apart from one another. It may perhaps seem that this reasoning applies only to the cases in which there *is* error, and that in true judgments (or in veridical perception) the content may still be the same as the *cognoscendum*. And if the term "true judgments" includes the mere awareness of an immediate datum, then in such judgments there is in fact no duality. But these constitute, at best, only a tiny part of the subject-matter of our claims to potential knowledge, the range of our possible judgments at any given time; and it is, indeed, an obviously inconvenient use of language to call them judgments at all. For the most part we are occupied, when judging, with matters conceived to be so related to us that we are not, from the very nature of that relation, necessarily immune against error; doubt as to the validity of our judgments about them is assumed to be not meaningless. But where error is *conceivable*, the relation between content and *cognoscendum* must be the same as in the case of actual error. The generic nature of judgments-potentially-erroneous must

be conceived in such a way as to permit the genus to have both judgments actually true and judgments actually false as its species— and to make it intelligible that the latter are aiming at the same mark as the former without hitting it. But a judgment is about something in particular; it has to do with a specific portion of reality. Since in actually erroneous judgments it is impossible that that portion can be the immediate datum, error must consist in attributing some character now present in perception or imagery, or represented by a verbal symbol, to *another* locus in reality, where it in fact is not present; and the species of actually true judgments will correspondingly be defined as the attribution of some such character to another locus in reality where it in fact *is* present. In all this, once more, I have only been putting explicitly the way of thinking about truth and error which seems to be common to all mankind, barring a few philosophers of more or less recent times. That bit of baldly dualistic epistemology known as the correspondence-theory of truth is one of the most deeply ingrained and persistent of human habits; there is much reason to doubt whether any of the philosophers who repudiate it actually dispense with it; yet *it* is not merely an instinctive faith, but has behind it certain simple and definite logical considerations which it appears absurd to deny. This also . . . may plausibly be supposed to have been a part of the unformulated working epistemology of our race from an early stage in the progress of intelligence; for there can hardly have been many featherless bipeds so naïve as not to have learned that man is liable to error, and so dull as to be unable to see, at least dimly, that in direct contemplation there is no room for error. . . .

. . . It is sufficient for the present definition of the nature and primary grounds of epistemological dualism to sum it up as a hypothetical proposition: *if* you postulate the externality of the entities to be known, in *any one* of the five ways in which it is asserted in the natural realistic creed—*i.e.*, spatial externality to the knower's body, temporal externality to the date of the event of perceiving or remembering, causal independence of that event, the identity of the the objects known by many observers, and the actual "otherness" of your neighbor's experience—then in that specific case your knowledge cannot be direct; the presented content upon which the knowledge depends must be numerically other than the thing which the knowledge is about, for one or more reasons given. And if you postulate externality in all five cases, then all your knowledge is indirect; the existents which convey it are not the existents which it means. . . .

CHARLES A. BAYLIS

Absolutism

*Charles A. Baylis (1902–   ) studied at the University of Washington
and Harvard, and has taught at Brown University, at the University of
Maryland, and since 1952 at Duke University. He is the author of* Formal
Logic *(with A. A. Bennett) (1938), and of* Ethics *(1958), and is now
working in the fields of metaphysics and epistemology.*

Bradley, Joachim, and idealists generally, have insisted on the
truth of the doctrine of the internality of relations. As Bradley [1]
expresses it, "Every relation essentially penetrates the being of its
terms and is in this sense intrinsical." Joachim [2] states it in the form,
"Every relation at least qualifies its terms, and is so far an adjective
of them." That "being an object of consciousness" is such an internal
relation, all idealists agree.

On the other hand, G. E. Moore [3] in England, R. B. Perry [4] in
America, and realists generally, have denied this doctrine and have
asserted that some relations are external, among them the relation of
"being an object of consciousness."

Here an impasse has been reached; neither side is convinced by
the other's arguments and after lengthy discussion both are of the
same opinion still. The object of this paper is to point a way out of
this impasse by establishing two points on which it should be
possible to bring both idealists and realists to agree: (*a*) In one
significant sense, a sense not even recognized by Moore in his
careful essay, the doctrine of the internality of relations is true, but
(*b*) this sense is not sufficient to warrant the conclusions the idealists have drawn from it. In particular it gives no support to either
idealism or absolutism.

1

Realists have tried to escape the doctrine of the internality of
relations by making a distinction between *all* the predicates or
characters of a term, i.e., its qualities, properties, and relations, and

From Charles A. Baylis, "Internality and Interdependence," *The Journal of
Philosophy,* XXVI (1929), 373–379. Reprinted by permission.

[1] *Appearance and Reality,* p. 392.
[2] *The Nature of Truth,* p. 11.
[3] *Philosophical Studies,* Ch. IX, pp. 276–309.
[4] *Present Philosophical Tendencies,* pp. 319 ff.

its *essential* characters. They then admit that a change in any relation of any entity changes some of the characters of that entity, since the relation changed is one such character. They deny, however, that any essential characters are necessarily changed. They assert that changes of some of the relations of some entities results in change of characters only accidental to those entities, and that such relations are therefore external.

To this, advocates of the internality of relations reply that all the characters of any entity are essential to it. An entity with even one different character is *ipso facto* not the same entity. But, the realists say, it is essentially the same, to which the idealists reply that it is very similar, but it is nevertheless essentially different just in respect of the character it doesn't have that the other does. And so another impasse is reached and the argument degenerates into a disagreement as to the validity of the distinction between essence and accident.

The realists insist that it is valid, at least pragmatically. For some purposes, those of action, for example, not all, but only some, of the characters of things are essential. As William James [5] puts it, *"the only meaning of essence is teleological, . . .* The essence of a thing is that one of its properties which is so *important for my interests* that in comparison with it I may neglect the rest."

Idealists quite willingly admit that the distinction between essence and accident is purely a pragmatic one, and they insist that just for this reason it has no theoretical validity. For the theoretical interest, for the philosophical purpose, the essence of any entity includes everything true of it, since the philosophical interest is the desire for complete knowledge, complete truth, and in relation to this desire *all* the characters of any entity are essential to it.

If this contention of the idealists be not admitted no solution of the problem is possible, for the idealists will insist on defining essence in terms of the intellectual interest, the realists in terms of other more practical interests. But it is conceivable that even pragmatists sometimes have the desire for complete knowledge. Caught in this mood they might admit the idealists' contention, at least long enough to see what follows from it. If so, the argument may proceed. Let it once be granted that (at least for some interests) all the characters of any entity are included in its essence, it is then possible to go on to the further question, what follows as to the truth and importance of the doctrine of the internality of relations.

[5] *Principles of Psychology*, Vol. II, p. 335. The italics are James's.

2

Any hope of an answer to this question would seem to require a reëxamination of the actual situation and a restatement of the problem in terms unprejudiced by long debate. Take a concrete example. A copy of Moore's *Philosophical Studies* now lying on my desk has many different characters, e.g., containing 342 pages, containing an essay on *External and Internal Relations,* being the recipient of light of a certain intensity, appearing to me a definite shade of dark blue-green, being five inches from a copy of Bradley's *Appearance and Reality,* exerting on this latter an attraction of a given force, and so on. For simplicity, assume a change in just one of these characters. Let the copy of *Appearance and Reality* be moved two inches nearer. The copy of *Philosophical Studies* now on my desk differs from the copy that was there a moment ago in at least one respect, namely, it has the character of being three inches from a copy of *Appearance and Reality,* whereas the copy of a moment ago was five inches from it. The change in this one character has also caused changes in other characters. The book now exerts a greater attraction on Bradley's book since the distance between them has been reduced; the lighting on it and its apparent color may be slightly changed, and so on. Other characters, however, have not changed as a result of its changed spatial relation to *Appearance and Reality.* It still contains 342 pages and an essay on *External and Internal Relations,* and so on.

If the original change had consisted in acquiring the character of being in contact with a flame, the other characters of my copy of *Philosophical Studies* would have undergone a much greater change. It might no longer contain 342 pages or an essay on *External and Internal Relations.* If, on the other hand, the original change had been one in the book's spatial relation to an invisible star in another astronomical universe some 11,000,000 light years away, the resultant effect on the other characters of the book would be very slight.

3

It is impossible that any change of any character of any entity should ever change all that entity's other characters. For even a cataclysmic change would leave intact, for example, the entity's character of having existed at one time, and its character of being able, under certain conditions, to be thought of. Contrariwise, it is impossible that any change of any character should ever fail to affect at least one of the other characters of that entity. For one of the characters of any entity is the character of having as characters, *a, b, c, d,* . . . No matter which of these characters, *a, b, c, d,* . . . is changed, the character of having as characters, *a, b, c, d,* . . . has also changed.

We may generalize, therefore, and conclude that it is a fact that *any change in any character of any entity entails some changes in some (never all) of the other characters of that entity.* This we may call the principle of the *partial interdependence* of the various characters of an entity. If this is what the doctrine of the internality of relations asserts, then that doctrine is true, and both realists and idealists should be willing to accept it.

4

Of course, the doctrine of the internality of relations might be taken as not asserting so much as the principle of partial interdependence, but merely as affirming that any character, *a,* of any entity, *X,* is internal to that entity in the sense that if *a* changes to *a',* *X* is different in just the respect that it no longer has the character *a* but the character *a'.* If so, the doctrine is obviously true, but entirely inefficacious. In regard to idealism, for example, it would entail only the consequence that an unperceived thing differs from a perceived thing in that it is not being perceived, an innocuous proposition that all would admit. If the doctrine of the internality of relations is to have any important consequences it must have more vigor than this specific form of the law of identity. This the principle of partial interdependence has. It asserts that the change of the character, *a,* of any entity, *X,* entails changes not only in the character, *a,* of that entity, but also in some of its other characters, *b* or *c* or *d.* . . . If the internality of relations is to be an important doctrine it must mean at least this. This principle of partial interdependence is true and it only remains to consider whether or not it is powerful enough to lead to the conclusions which the internality of relations has been thought to imply, namely, idealism and absolutism.

5

In the first place, the principle of partial interdependence tells us that a change of any character of any entity entails changes in some of the other characters of that entity, but it doesn't tell us in which ones. To answer any specific question as to whether a change of character *a* entails a change of character *b* we must turn, not to our principle, but to a specific study of the two characters in question. Does *a* have any causal relation to *b*? Does *a* have any implicational relation to *b*? Does *a* have any other type of necessary connection with *b*? Only by answering such specific questions can we know whether a change of any given character will result in a change of any other given character.

This consideration makes it evident that the principle of partial interdependence does not imply idealism. It implies merely that when an entity loses the character of "being an object of consciousness," changes in some of its other characters result. But what other characters are changed the principle does not tell us; we must discover that by examination of this particular situation. Usually, for example, an entity, when it ceases to be perceived by a given organism, has different gravitational relations to that organism than it had when it was perceived, for non-perception usually follows a bodily movement, e.g., the turning away of the head or eyes. But the vital question at issue between realism and idealism still remains. Were the entity's secondary qualities, its primary qualities, its existence, affected by the loss of the character of being perceived? Is the loss of these characters causally or implicationally connected with the loss of perception? Certainly the principle of the partial interdependence of characters can not answer these questions. For from that principle no implicational relation between these particular given characters may be inferred. If such a relation exists it can be known only on other grounds. Furthermore, a causal relation between the loss of these characters and the loss of perception could only be discovered by empirical observation and comparison of the perceived entity with the same entity unperceived. And, since the latter, by the very nature of the case, can not be empirically examined, the question whether or no the loss of perception causally results in the loss of these other characters seems forever unanswerable. As far, then, as the principle of partial interdependence goes, the loss of an entity's primary or secondary qualities or its existence does not necessarily follow the loss of its relation of "being an object of consciousness." As far as this principle is concerned either realism or idealism might be true.

6

Nor does the principle of partial interdependence imply absolutism. When my copy of *Appearance and Reality* is moved two inches closer to my copy of *Philosophical Studies* the gravitational and perhaps the electro-magnetic properties of both books and of all other physical objects in the universe are slightly changed. True, but what of it? Some of the characters of both books are still the same, e.g., their contents and the meanings of them. If each thing is related to every other thing, it follows from this together with the principle of partial interdependence that a change of any character of anything produces changes in some of the characters of all things. But what absolutism requires [6] is that any change should produce changes in all the characters of all things, and not the truth but the falsity of this is implied by the *partial* interdependence of characters. For this means that no change ever affects *all* the characters of anything. Some changes of some characters affect many characters; some changes of some characters affect few characters; and hence, certainly, some changes leave entirely unaffected many characters of many things.

If, then, the principle of partial interdependence is what is meant by the internality of relations, that doctrine is true, but the important conclusions which idealists have drawn from it, idealism and absolutism, do not follow. Of course, this does not disprove these views, for idealists advance other and independent grounds for them. They do not, however, follow from the principle of partial interdependence.

8

This paper attempted to contribute this one step toward the solution of the internality of relations controversy: The partial interdependence of the characters of an entity is one important possible interpretation of the doctrine of the internality of relations. It includes what that doctrine on the face of it seems to assert. If that doctrine means what this principle includes, then it is true but irrelevant to the proof of either idealism or absolutism.

It is suggested that the doggedness with which idealists have maintained the internality of relations is due to the undeniable

[6] The requirement of absolutism has usually been stated in the ambiguous form: any change affects everything. But this might mean either: (1) any change of any character of anything entails changes in some characters of all things, or (2) any change of any character of .anything entails changes in all the characters of all things. If (1) is meant, it is true but unimportant, for it would still be true that some changes leave unaffected many characters of many things. If (2) is meant it would be important if true, but as explained above, it is false.

truth of the principle of partial interdependence, and that the acerbity with which realists have denied the former is due to conclusions which idealists have drawn from it which do not follow from the latter.

If the idealists wish to maintain that the internality of relations means something other than this principle, something with more teeth to it, then it is incumbent upon them to distinguish this meaning clearly and to show that its truth comes to it independently and not merely by transfer due to association with the true principle of partial interdependence.

PART II

Basic Metaphysical Concepts

ARISTOTLE

Substance

*Aristotle (384–322 B.C.), pupil of Plato and tutor of Alexander, authored
a host of philosophical and other volumes and did much to create classical
logic and biology. His* Metaphysics *has given both name and substance
to that central field of philosophy which is the subject of this volume.
His influence on philosophic thought for thousands of years has been deep
and extensive.*

Substance, in the truest and primary and most definite sense of
the word, is that which is neither predicable of a subject nor
present in a subject; for instance, the individual man or horse. But
in a secondary sense those things are called substances within
which, as species, the primary substances are included; also those
which, as genera, include the species. For instance, the individual
man is included in the species 'man', and the genus to which the
species belongs is 'animal'; these, therefore—that is to say, the
species 'man' and the genus 'animal'—are termed secondary substances.

It is plain from what has been said that both the name and the
definition of the predicate must be predicable of the subject. For
instance, 'man' is predicated of the individual man. Now in this
case the name of the species 'man' is applied to the individual, for
we use the term 'man' in describing the individual; and the definition of 'man' will also be predicated of the individual man, for the
individual man is both man and animal. Thus, both the name and
the definition of the species are predicable of the individual.

From W. D. Ross (ed.), *The Works of Aristotle* (Oxford: Clarendon Press,
1928), Vol. I. Used by permission of the Clarendon Press, Oxford. The selection
is taken from *Categories,* Chap. 5, pp. 2a11–2b17.

With regard, on the other hand, to those things which are present in a subject, it is generally the case that neither their name nor their definition is predicable of that in which they are present. Though, however, the definition is never predicable, there is nothing in certain cases to prevent the name being used. For instance, 'white' being present in a body is predicated of that in which it is present, for a body is called white: the definition, however, of the colour 'white' is never predicable of the body.[1]

Everything except primary substances is either predicable of a primary substance or present in a primary substance. This becomes evident by reference to particular instances which occur. 'Animal' is predicated of the species 'man', therefore of the individual man, for if there were no individual man of whom it could be predicated, it could not be predicated of the species 'man' at all. Again, colour is present in body, therefore in individual bodies, for if there were no individual body in which it was present, it could not be present in body at all. Thus everything except primary substances is either predicated of primary substances, or is present in them, and if these last did not exist, it would be impossible for anything else to exist.

Of secondary substances, the species is more truly substance than the genus, being more nearly related to primary substance. For if any one should render an account of what a primary substance is, he would render a more instructive account, and one more proper to the subject, by stating the species than by stating the genus. Thus, he would give a more instructive account of an individual man by stating that he was man than by stating that he was animal, for the former description is peculiar to the individual in a greater degree, while the latter is too general. Again, the man who gives an account of the nature of an individual tree will give a more instructive account by mentioning the species 'tree' than by mentioning the genus 'plant'.

Moreover, primary substances are most properly called substances in virtue of the fact that they are the entities which underlie everything else, and that everything else is either predicated of them or present in them.

---

[1] Qualities pure and simple are abstractions, and in their abstract substantival form, with regard to which they are defined, do not form the predicate of substances. We do not say 'X is whiteness' but 'X is white'. It is to this latter use of the adjective that Aristotle refers when he says that 'the name is sometimes applicable'; for in Greek 'whiteness' is not only λευκότης, but also τὸ λευκόν. In English 'evil' used in the one case as a noun, in the other as an adjective, would afford a parallel.—Ed.

The Identity of Indiscernibles

Gottfried Wilhelm von Leibniz (1646–1716) is said by Russell to be "one of the supreme intellects of all time." The present selection from his writings is indicative of his doctrine of substance, of his thoroughgoing determinism, and of his famous principle of the identity of indiscernibles.

Remarks on the letter of M. Arnaud touching on my proposition: that the individual notion of each person includes once for all everything that will ever happen to him.

It is necessary to philosophize differently about the concept of an individual substance than about the species-like concept of a sphere [in general]. For the notion of a species includes only those eternal or necessary truths [applicable to all its members], whereas the concept of an individual includes . . . all that which is true of it as a matter of fact or relates it to existence and to time. . . . Also the notion of a sphere in general is incomplete and abstract, that is to say that one considers only the essence of a sphere in general or in theory without regard to particular circumstances. . . . But the notion of the sphere that Archimedes had placed on his tomb is complete and must include everything which pertains to that particular thing of that kind. . . . In addition to the form of this sphere there enters into the notion of it consideration of the matter of which it is made, the place, the time and the circumstances, which by a continuing concatenation of events would finally envelop all the subsequent events in the universe, if one could follow through all that these notions include. For the notion of this bit of matter of which this sphere is made includes every change which it has undergone and will one day undergo. Thus, according to me, every individual substance contains impressions of all that has ever happened to it and marks of everything which ever will occur to it. . . .

. . . The nature of an individual must be complete and determinate. I am even very much persuaded of that which St. Thomas has

From a letter to Hessen-Rheinfels (May, 1686), reprinted in *Die philosophischen Schriften* of *Gottfried Wilhelm von Leibniz*, ed. C. J. Gerhardt, Zweiter Band, Berlin, Weidmannsche Buchhandlung, 1879), pp. 37–47. Translated by C. A. Baylis.

already taught with regard to intelligences, and which I hold to be true in general, namely that is is impossible that there should be two individuals entirely alike or different only numerically. . . .

. . . Since we suppose that it is the same individual substance which endures, or rather is I, who subsists during the time AB and who am then in Paris, and which is still I who subsists during the time BC and who is then in Germany, it is absolutely necessary that there be a reason which makes it true to say that we endure, that is that I who have been in Paris, am now in Germany. For if there were no reason one would have as much right to say that it is [not I but] another. It is true that my introspective experience has convinced me *a posteriori* of this identity, but it is necessary that there be also a reason *a priori*. It is impossible to find any other than that both my attributes of the earlier time and state and my attributes of the later time and state are predicates of one and the same subject. Now what is it to say that the predicate is in the subject, if not that the notion of the predicate finds itself in some manner included in the notion of the subject? And since from the time that I commenced to be, one could truly say of me that this or that would happen to me, it is necessary to avow that these predicates are laws enclosed in the subject, or in the complete concept of me, which determines that which one calls me, which is the basis of the connection of all my different states and which God knew perfectly through all eternity.

. . . In saying that the individual notion of Adam includes all that will ever happen to him I wish to say nothing other than what all philosophers understand in saying that the predicate is contained in the subject of all true propositions.

MAX BLACK

The Identity of Indiscernibles

Max Black (1909–   ), *born in Baku, student at Queens College, Cambridge, Göttingen and London, has been at Cornell since 1946, Sage Professor there since 1954. Author of many books and articles, editor and translator of others, President American Philosophical Association (Eastern Division) 1958, he has been in the thick of philosophical discussions for many years. The article reprinted here originated in argument with A. J. Ayer at a Philosophical Association meeting.*

A. The principle of the Identity of Indiscernibles seems to me obviously true. And I don't see how we are going to define identity or establish the connexion between mathematics and logic without using it.

B. It seems to me obviously false. And your troubles as a mathematical logician are beside the point. If the principle is false you have no right to use it.

A. You simply *say* it's false—and even if you said so three times that wouldn't make it so.

B. Well, you haven't done anything more yourself than assert the principle to be true. As Bradley once said, "Assertion can demand no more than counter-assertion; and what is affirmed on the one side, we on the other can simply deny".

A. How will this do for an argument? If two things, *a* and *b*, are given, the first has the property of being identical with *a*. Now *b* cannot have this property, for else *b* would be *a*, and we should have only one thing, not two as assumed. Hence *a* has at least one property, which *b* does not have, that is to say the property of being identical with *a*.

B. This is a roundabout way of saying nothing, for "*a* has the property of being identical with *a*" means no more than "*a* is *a*". When you begin to say "*a* is . . ." I am supposed to know what thing you are referring to as '*a*' and I expect to be told something about that thing. But when you end the sentence with the words ". . . is *a*" I am left still waiting. The sentence "*a* is *a*" is a useless tautology.

From Max Black, "The Identity of Indiscernibles," *Mind,* **LXI** (1952), 153–163. Used by permission of the author and of the editor of *Mind.*

A. Are you as scornful about difference as about identity? For
a also has, and *b* does not have, the property of being different from
b. This is a second property that the one thing has but not the
other.

B. All you are saying is that *b* is different from *a*. I think the
form of words "*a* is different from *b*" does have the advantage
over "*a* is *a*" that it might be used to give information. I might learn
from hearing it used that '*a*' and '*b*' were applied to different things.
But this is not what you want to say, since you are trying to use
the names, not mention them. When I already know what '*a*' and '*b*'
stand for, "*a* is different from *b*" tells me nothing. It, too, is a useless
tautology.

A. I wouldn't have expected you to treat 'tautology' as a term of
abuse. Tautology or not, the sentence has a philosophical use. It
expresses the necessary truth that different things have at least one
property not in common. Thus different things must be discernible;
and hence, by contraposition, indiscernible things must be identical.
Q.E.D.

B. Why obscure matters by this old-fashioned language? By
"indiscernible" I suppose you mean the same as "having all properties in common". Do you claim to have proved that two things
having all their properties in common are identical?

A. Exactly.

B. Then this is a poor way of stating your conclusion. If *a* and *b*
are identical, there is just one thing having the two names '*a*' and
'*b*'; and in that case it is absurd to say that *a* and *b* are two. Conversely, once you have supposed there are *two* things having all
their properties in common, you can't without contradicting yourself
say that *they* are "identical".

A. I can't believe you were really misled. I simply meant to say
it is logically impossible for two things to have all their properties
in common. I showed that *a* must have at least two properties—
the property of being identical with *a*, and the property of being
different from *b*—neither of which can be a property of *b*. Doesn't
this prove the principle of Identity of Indiscernibles?

B. Perhaps you have proved something. If so, the nature of your
proof should show us exactly what you have proved. If you want to
call "being identical with *a*" a "property," I suppose I can't prevent
you. But you must then accept the consequences of this way of
talking. All you mean when you say "*a* has the property of being
identical with *a*" is that *a* is *a*. And all you mean when you say "*b*

does not have the property of being identical with *a*" is that *b* is not *a*. So what you have "proved" is that *a* is *a* and *b* is not *a*, that is to say, *b* and *a* are different. Similarly, when you said that *a*, but not *b*, had the property of being different from *b*, you were simply saying that *a* and *b* were different. In fact you are merely redescribing the hypothesis that *a* and *b* are different by calling it a case of "difference of properties". Drop the misleading description and your famous principle reduces to the truism that different things are different. How true! And how uninteresting!

A. Well, the properties of identity and difference may be uninteresting, but they *are* properties. If I had shown that grass was green, I suppose you would say I hadn't shown that grass was coloured.

B. You certainly would not have shown that grass had any colour *other than* green.

A. What it comes to is that you object to the conclusion of my argument *following* from the premise that *a* and *b* are different.

B. No, I object to the triviality of the conclusion. If you want to have an interesting principle to defend, you must interpret "property" more narrowly—enough so, at any rate, for "identity" and "difference" not to count as properties.

A. Your notion of an interesting principle seems to be one which I shall have difficulty in establishing. Will you at least allow me to include among "properties" what are sometimes called "relational characteristics"—like *being married to Caesar* or *being at a distance from London?*

B. Why not? If you are going to defend the principle, it is for you to decide what version you wish to defend.

A. In that case, I don't need to count identity and difference as properties. Here is a different argument that seems to me quite conclusive. The only way we can discover that two different things exist is by finding out that one has a quality not possessed by the other or else that one has a relational characteristic that the other hasn't. . . .

B. [But] isn't it logically possible that the universe should have contained nothing but two exactly similar spheres? We might suppose that each was made of chemically pure iron, had a diameter of one mile, that they had the same temperature, colour, and so on, and that nothing else existed. Then every quality and relational characteristic of the one would also be a property of the other. Now if what I am describing is logically possible, it is not impossible for

two things to have all their properties in common. This seems to me
to *refute* the Principle.

A. Your supposition, I repeat, isn't verifiable and therefore can't
be regarded as meaningful. But supposing you *have* described a
possible world, I still don't see that you have refuted the principle.
Consider one of the spheres, *a*, . . .

B. How can I, since there is no way of telling them apart? *Which*
one do you want me to consider?

A. This is very foolish. I mean either of the two spheres, leaving
you to decide which one you wished to consider. If I were to say to
you "Take any book off the shelf" it would be foolish on your part
to reply "Which?"

B. It's a poor analogy. I know how to take a book off a shelf, but
I don't know how to identify one of two spheres supposed to be
alone in space and so symmetrically placed with respect to each
other that neither has any quality or character the other does not
also have.

A. All of which goes to show as I said before, the unverifiability
of your supposition. Can't you imagine that one sphere has been
designated as '*a*'?

B. I can imagine only what is logically possible. Now it is logically
possible that somebody should enter the universe I have described,
see one of the spheres on his left hand and proceed to call it '*a*'. I
can imagine that all right, if that's enough to satisfy you.

A. Very well, now let me try to finish what I begin to say about
a . . .

B. I still can't let you, because you, in your present situation, have
no right to talk about *a*. All I have conceded is that if something
were to happen to introduce a change into my universe, so that an
observer entered and could see the two spheres, one of them could
then have a name. But this would be a different supposition from
the one I wanted to consider. My spheres don't yet have names.
If an observer were to enter the scene, he could perhaps put a red
mark on one of the spheres. You might just as well say "By '*a*' I
mean the sphere which would be the first to be marked by a red
mark if anyone were to arrive and were to proceed to make a red
mark!" You might just as well ask me to consider the first daisy in
my lawn that would be picked by a child, if a child were to come
along and do the picking. This doesn't now distinguish any daisy
from the others. You are just pretending to use a name.

A. And I think you are just pretending not to understand me.

All I am asking you to do is to think of one of your spheres, no matter which, so that I may go on to say something about it when you give me a chance.

B. You talk as if naming an object and then thinking about it were the easiest thing in the world. But it isn't so easy. Suppose I tell you to name any spider in my garden: if you can catch one first or describe one uniquely you can name it easily enough. But you can't pick one out, let alone "name" it by just thinking. You remind me of the mathematicians who thought that talking about an Axiom of Choice would really allow them to choose a single member of a collection when they had no criterion of choice.

A. At this rate you will never give me a chance to say anything. Let me try to make my point without using names. Each of the spheres will surely differ from the other in being at some distance from that other one, but at no distance from itself—that is to say, it will bear at least one relation to itself—*being at no distance from,* or *being in the same place as*—that it does not bear to the other. And this will serve to distinguish it from the other.

B. Not at all. *Each* will have the relational characteristic *being at a distance of two miles,* say, *from the centre of a sphere one mile in diameter,* etc. And each will have the relational characteristic (if you want to call it that) of *being in the same place as itself.* The two are alike in this respect as in all others.

A. But look here. Each sphere occupies a different place; and this at least will distinguish them from one another.

B. This sounds as if you thought the places had some independent existence, though I don't suppose you really think so. To say the spheres are in "different places" is just to say that there is a distance between the two spheres; and we have already seen that will not serve to distinguish them. Each is at a distance—indeed the same distance—from the other.

A. When I said they were at different places I didn't mean simply that they were at a distance from one another. That one sphere is in a certain place does not entail the existence of any *other* sphere. So to say that one sphere is in its place, and the other in its place, and then to add that these places are different seems to me different from saying the spheres are at a distance from one another.

B. What does it mean to say "a sphere is in its place"? Nothing at all, so far as I can see. Where else could it be? *All* you are saying is that the spheres are in different places.

A. Then my retort is, What does it mean to say "Two spheres are in different places"? Or, as you so neatly put it, "Where else could they be?"

B. You have a point. What I should have said was that your assertion that the spheres occupied different places said nothing at all, unless you were drawing attention to the necessary truth that different physical objects must be in different places. Now if two spheres must be in different places, as indeed they must, to say that the spheres occupy different places is to say no more than they are two spheres.

A. This is like a point you made before. You won't allow me to deduce anything from the supposition that there are two spheres.

B. Let me put it another way. In the two-sphere universe, the only reason for saying that the places occupied were different would be that different things occupied them. So in order to show the places were different you would first have to show, in some other way, that the spheres were different. You will never be able to distinguish the spheres by means of the places they occupy.

A. A minute ago, you were willing to allow that somebody might give your spheres different names. Will you let me suppose that some traveller has visited your monotonous "universe" and has named one sphere "Castor" and the other "Pollux"?

B. All right—provided you don't try to use those names yourself.

A. Wouldn't the traveller, at least, have to recognise that *being at a distance of two miles from Castor* was not the same property as being at a distance of two miles *from Pollux*?

B. I don't see why. If he were to see that Castor and Pollux had exactly the same properties, he would see that "being at a distance of two miles from Castor" meant exactly the same as "being at a distance of two miles from Pollux".

A. They couldn't mean the same. If they did, *"being at a distance of two miles from Castor and at the same time not being at a distance of two miles from Pollux"* would be a self-contradictory description. But plenty of bodies could answer to this description. Again if the two expressions meant the same, anything which was two miles from Castor would have to be two miles from Pollux—which is clearly false. So the two expressions don't mean the same and the two spheres have at least two properties not in common.

B. Which?

A. *Being at a distance of two miles from Castor* and *being at a distance of two miles from Pollux.*

B. But now you are *using* the words "Castor" and "Pollux" as if they really stood for something. They are just our old friends 'a' and 'b' in disguise.

A. You surely don't want to say that the arrival of the name-giving traveller creates spatial properties? Perhaps we can't name your spheres and therefore can't name the corresponding properties; but the properties must be there.

B. What can this mean? The traveller has not visited the spheres, and the spheres have no names—neither 'Castor', nor 'Pollux', nor 'a', nor 'b', nor any others. Yet you still want to say they have certain properties which cannot be referred to without using names for the spheres. You want to say "the property of being at a distance from Castor" though it is logically impossible for you to talk in this way. You can't speak, but you won't be silent.

A. How eloquent, and how unconvincing! But since you seem to have convinced yourself, at least, perhaps you can explain another thing that bothers me: I don't see that you have a right to talk as you do about places or spatial relations in connexion with your so-called "universe". So long as we are talking about our own universe—*the* universe—I know what you mean by "distance", "diameter", "place" and so on. But in what you want to call a universe, even though it contains only two objects, I don't see what such words could mean. So far as I can see, you are applying these spatial terms in their present usage to a hypothetical situation which contradicts the presuppositions of that usage.

B. What do you mean by "presupposition"?

A. Well, you spoke of measured distances, for one thing. Now this presupposes some means of measurement. Hence your "universe" must contain at least a third thing—a ruler or some other measuring device.

B. Are you claiming that a universe must have at least three things in it? What is the least number of things required to make a world?

A. No, all I am saying is that you cannot describe a configuration as *spatial* unless it includes at least three objects. This is part of the meaning of "spatial"—and it is no more mysterious than saying you can't have a game of chess without there existing at least thirty-five things (thirty-two pieces, a chess board, and two players).

B. If this is all that bothers you, I can easily provide for three or any number of things without changing the force of my counter-example. The important thing, for my purpose, was that the configuration of two spheres was symmetrical. So long as we preserve this feature of the imaginary universe, we can now allow any number of objects to be found in it.

A. You mean any *even* number of objects.

B. Quite right. Why not imagine a plane running clear through space, with everything that happens on one side of it always exactly duplicated at an equal distance in the other side.

A. A kind of cosmic mirror producing real images.

B. Yes, except that there wouldn't be any mirror! The point is that in *this* world we can imagine any degree of complexity and change to occur. No reason to exclude rulers, compasses, and weighing machines. No reason, for that matter, why the Battle of Waterloo shouldn't happen.

A. Twice over, you mean—with Napoleon surrendering later in two different places simultaneously!

B. Provided you wanted to call both of them "Napoleon".

A. So your point is that everything could be duplicated on the other side of the non-existent Looking Glass. I suppose whenever a man got married, his identical twin would be marrying the identical twin of the first man's fiancée?

B. Exactly.

A. Except that "identical twins" wouldn't be *numerically* identical?

B. You seem to be agreeing with me.

A. Far from it. This is just a piece of gratuitous metaphysics. If the inhabitants of your world had enough sense to know what was sense and what wasn't, they would never suppose all the events in their world were duplicated. It would be much more sensible for them to regard the "second" Napoleon as a mere mirror image—and similarly for all the other supposed "duplicates."

B. But they could walk through the "mirror" and find water just as wet, sugar just as sweet, and grass just as green on the other side.

A. You don't understand me. They would not postulate "another side". A man looking at the "mirror" would be seeing *himself*, not a duplicate. If he walked in a straight line toward the "mirror" he would eventually find himself back at his starting point, not at a duplicate of his starting point. This would involve their having a different geometry from ours—but that would be preferable to the logician's nightmare of the reduplicated universe.

B. They might think so—until the twins really began to behave differently for the first time!

A. Now it's you who are tinkering with your supposition. You can't have your universe and change it too.

B. All right, I retract.

A. The more I think about your "universe" the queerer it seems. What would happen when a man crossed your invisible "mirror"? While he was actually crossing, his body would have to change shape, in order to preserve the symmetry. Would it gradually shrink to nothing and then expand again?

B. I confess I hadn't thought of that.

A. And here is something that explodes the whole notion. Would you say that one of the two Napoleons in your universe had his heart in the right place—literally, I mean?

B. Why, of course.

A. In that case his "mirror-image" twin would have the heart on the opposite side of the body. One Napoleon would have his heart on the left of his body, and the other would have it on the right of his body.

B. It's a good point, though it would still make objects like spheres indistinguishable. But let me try again. Let me abandon the original idea of a *plane* of symmetry and to suppose instead that we have only a *centre* of symmetry. I mean that everything that happened at any place would be exactly duplicated at a place an equal distance on the opposite side of the centre of symmetry. In short, the universe would be what the mathematicians call "radially symmetrical". And to avoid complications we could sup- pose that the centre of symmetry itself was physically inaccessible, so that it would be impossible for any material body to pass through it. Now in *this* universe, identical twins would have to be either both right-handed or both left-handed.

A. Your universes are beginning to be as plentiful as blackberries. You are too ingenious to see the force of my argument about verifiability. Can't you see that your supposed description of a universe in which everything has its "identical twin" doesn't describe anything verifiably different from a corresponding universe without such duplication? This must be so, no matter what kind of symmetry your universe manifested.

B. You are assuming that in order to verify that there are two things of a certain kind, it must be possible to show that one has a property not possessed by the other. But this is not so. A pair of very close but similar magnetic poles produce a characteristic field of force which assures me that there are two poles, even if I have no way of examining them separately. The presence of two exactly similar stars at a great distance might be detected by some resultant gravitational effect or by optical interference—or in some such sim-ilar way—even though we had no way of inspecting one in isolation from the other. Don't physicists say something like this about the electrons inside an atom? We can verify *that* there are two, that is to say a certain property of the whole configuration, even though there is no way of detecting any character that uniquely characterises any element of the configuration.

A. But if you were to approach your two stars one would have to be on your left and one on the right. And this would distinguish them.

B. I agree. Why shouldn't we say that the two stars are dis-tinguishable—meaning that it would be possible for an observer to see one on his left and the other on his right, or more generally, that it would be *possible* for one star to come to have a relation to a third object that the second star would not have to that third object.

A. So you agree with me after all.

B. Not if you mean that the two stars do not have all their prop-erties in common. All I said was that it was logically possible for them to enter into different relationships with a third object. But this would be a change in the universe.

A. If you are right, nothing unobserved would be observable. For the presence of an observer would always change it, and the observation would always be an observation of something else.

B. I don't say that every observation changes what is observed. My point is that there isn't any *being to the right* or *being to the left* in the two-sphere universe until an observer is introduced, that is to say until a real change is made.

A. But the spheres themselves wouldn't have changed.

B. Indeed they would: they would have acquired new relational characteristics. In the absence of any asymmetric observer, I repeat, the spheres would have all their properties in common (including, if you like, the power to enter into different relations with other objects). Hence the principle of Identity of Indiscernibles is false.

A. So perhaps you really do have twenty hands after all?

B. Not a bit of it. Nothing that I have said prevents me from holding that we can verify *that* there are exactly two. But we could know *that* two things existed without there being any way to dis-tinguish one from the other. The Principle is false.

A. I am not surprised that you ended in this way, since you assumed it in the description of your fantastic "universe". Of course, if you began by assuming that the spheres were numerically different though qualitatively alike, you could end by "proving" what you first assumed.

B. But I wasn't "proving" anything. I tried to support my contention that it is logically possible for two things to have all their properties in common by giving an illustrative description. (Similarly, if I had to show it is logically possible for nothing at all to be seen I would ask you to imagine a universe in which everybody was blind.) It was for you to show that my description concealed some hidden contradiction. And you haven't done so.

A. All the same I am not convinced.

B. Well, then, you ought to be.

Universals

Willard Van Orman Quine (*1908–*   ), *student at Oberlin and Harvard, teacher at Harvard since 1936, past President of Association for Symbolic Logic and American Philosophical Association* (*Eastern Division*), *is a logician and philosopher of distinction. Long a nominalist, seeking ways of avoiding commitment to abstract entities, he has finally, in his* Word and Object (*1960*), *admitted classes to his ontology.*

Now let us turn to the ontological problem of universals: the question whether there are such entities as attributes, relations, classes, numbers, functions. McX, characteristically enough, thinks there are. Speaking of attributes, he says: "There are red houses, red roses, red sunsets; this much is prephilosophical common sense in which we must all agree. These houses, roses, and sunsets, then, have something in common; and this which they have in common is all I mean by the attribute of redness." For McX, thus, there being attributes is even more obvious and trivial than the obvious and trivial fact of there being red houses, roses, and sunsets. This, I think, is characteristic of metaphysics, or at least of that part of metaphysics called ontology: one who regards a statement on this subject as true at all must regard it as trivially true. One's ontology is basic to the conceptual scheme by which he interprets all experiences, even the most commonplace ones. Judged within some particular conceptual scheme—and how else is judgment possible?—an ontological statement goes without saying, standing in need of no separate justification at all. Ontological statements follow immediately from all manner of casual statements of commonplace fact, just as—from the point of view, anyway, of McX's conceptual scheme—'There is an attribute' follows from 'There are red houses, red roses, red sunsets'.

Judged in another conceptual scheme, an ontological statement which is axiomatic to McX's mind may, with equal immediacy and triviality, be adjudged false. One may admit that there are red houses, roses, and sunsets, but deny, except as a popular and mis-

---

leading manner of speaking, that they have anything in common. The words 'houses', 'roses', and 'sunsets' are true of sundry individual entities which are houses and roses and sunsets, and the word 'red' or 'red object' is true of each of sundry individual entities which are red houses, red roses, red sunsets; but there is not, in addition, any entity whatever, individual or otherwise, which is named by the word 'redness', nor, for that matter, by the word 'househood', 'rosehood', 'sunsethood'. That the houses and roses and sunsets are all of them red may be taken as ultimate and irreducible, and it may be held that McX is no better off, in point of real explanatory power, for all the occult entities which he posits under such names as 'redness'.

One means by which McX might naturally have tried to impose his ontology of universals on us was already removed before we turned to the problem of universals. McX cannot argue that predicates such as 'red' or 'is-red', which we all concur in using, must be regarded as names each of a single universal entity in order that they be meaningful at all. For we have seen that being a name of something is a much more special feature than being meaningful. He cannot even charge us—at least not by *that* argument—with having posited an attribute of pegasizing by our adoption of the predicate 'pegasizes'.

However, McX hits upon a different stratagem. "Let us grant," he says, "this distinction between meaning and naming of which you make so much. Let us even grant that 'is red', 'pegasizes', etc., are not names of attributes. Still, you admit they have meanings. But these *meanings*, whether they are *named* or not, are still universals, and I venture to say that some of them might even be the very things that I call attributes, or something to much the same purpose in the end."

For McX, this is an unusually penetrating speech; and the only way I know to counter it is by refusing to admit meanings. However, I feel no reluctance toward refusing to admit meanings, for I do not thereby deny that words and statements are meaningful. McX and I may agree to the letter in our classification of linguistic forms into the meaningful and the meaningless, even though McX construes meaningfulness as the *having* (in some sense of 'having') of some abstract entity which he calls a meaning, whereas I do not. I remain free to maintain that the fact that a given linguistic utterance is meaningful (or *significant*, as I prefer to say so as not to invite hypostasis of meanings as entities) is an ultimate and irreducible matter of fact; or, I may undertake to analyze it in terms directly of what people do in the presence of the linguistic utterance in question and other utterances similar to it.

The useful ways in which people ordinarily talk or seem to talk about meanings boil down to two: the *having* of meanings, which is significance, and *sameness* of meaning, or synonymy. What is called *giving* the meaning of an utterance is simply the uttering of a synonym, couched, ordinarily, in clearer language than the original. If we are allergic to meanings as such, we can speak directly of utterances as significant or insignificant, and as synonymous or heteronymous one with another. The problem of explaining these adjectives 'significant' and 'synonymous' with some degree of clarity and rigor—preferably, as I see it, in terms of behavior—is as difficult as it is important. But the explanatory value of special and irreducible intermediary entities called meanings is surely illusory.

Up to now I have argued that we can use singular terms significantly in sentences without presupposing that there are the entities which those terms purport to name. I have argued further that we can use general terms, for example, predicates, without conceding them to be names of abstract entities. I have argued further that we can view utterances as significant, and as synonymous or heteronymous with one another, without countenancing a realm of entities called meanings. At this point McX begins to wonder whether there is any limit at all to our ontological immunity. Does *nothing* we may say commit us to the assumption of universals or other entities which we may find unwelcome?

I have already suggested a negative answer to this question, in speaking of bound variables, or variables of quantification,[1] in connection with Russell's theory of descriptions. We can very easily involve ourselves in ontological commitments by saying, for example, that *there is something* (bound variable) which red houses and sunsets have in common; or that *there is something* which is a prime number larger than a million. But this is, essentially, the *only* way we can involve ourselves in ontological commitments: by our use of bound variables. The use of alleged names is no criterion, for we can repudiate their namehood at the drop of a hat unless the assumption of a corresponding entity can be spotted in the things

---

[1] By "bound variables" or "variables of quantification" Quine is referring to such expressions as "for everything, x" or "there exists at least one thing, x". The former is often symbolized "(x)", the latter "$(\exists x)$".—Ed.

we affirm in terms of bound variables. Names are, in fact, altogether immaterial to the ontological issue, for I have shown, in connection with 'Pegasus' and 'pegasize',[2] that names can be converted to descriptions, and Russell has shown that descriptions can be eliminated. Whatever we say with the help of names can be said in a language which shuns names altogether. To be assumed as an entity is, purely and simply, to be reckoned as the value of a variable. In terms of the categories of traditional grammar, this amounts roughly to saying that to be is to be in the range of reference of a pronoun. Pronouns are the basic media of reference; nouns might better have been named propronouns. The variables of quantification, 'something', 'nothing', 'everything', range over our whole ontology, whatever it may be; and we are convicted of a particular ontological presupposition if, and only if, the alleged presuppositum has to be reckoned among the entities over which our variables range in order to render one of our affirmations true.

We may say, for example, that some dogs are white and not thereby commit ourselves to recognizing either doghood or whiteness as entities. 'Some dogs are white' says that some things that are dogs are white; and, in order that this statement be true, the things over which the bound variable 'something' ranges must include some white dogs, but need not include doghood or whiteness. On the other hand, when we say that some zoölogical species are cross-fertile we are committing ourselves to recognizing as entities the several species themselves, abstract though they are. We remain so committed at least until we devise some way of so paraphrasing the statement as to show that the seeming reference to species on the part of our bound variable was an avoidable manner of speaking.

Classical mathematics, as the example of primes larger than a million clearly illustrates, is up to its neck in commitments to an ontology of abstract entities. Thus it is that the great mediaeval controversy over universals has flared up anew in the modern philosophy of mathematics. The issue is clearer now than of old, because we now have a more explicit standard whereby to decide what ontology a given theory or form of discourse is committed to: a theory is committed to those and only those entities to which the

---

[2] Quine points out that we can always eliminate the apparent reference of a proper name such as "Pegasus" by replacing it by a definite description such as, "the thing that *is-Pegasus*" or "the thing that *pegasizes*." Then such a statement as "Pegasus has wings" becomes "there exists one and only one *x* such that *x* pegasizes and *x* has wings."—Ed.

bound variables of the theory must be capable of referring in order that the affirmations made in the theory be true.

Because this standard of ontological presupposition did not emerge clearly in the philosophical tradition, the modern philosophical mathematicians have not on the whole recognized that they were debating the same old problem of universals in a newly clarified form. But the fundamental cleavages among modern points of view on foundations of mathematics do come down pretty explicitly to disagreements as to the range of entities to which the bound variables should be permitted to refer.

The three main mediaeval points of view regarding universals are designated by historians as *realism, conceptualism,* and *nominalism.* Essentially these same three doctrines reappear in twentieth-century surveys of the philosophy of mathematics under the new names *logicism, intuitionism,* and *formalism.*

Realism, as the word is used in connection with the mediaeval controversy over universals, is the Platonic doctrine that universals or abstract entities have being independently of the mind; the mind may discover them but cannot create them. *Logicism,* represented by Frege, Russell, Whitehead, Church, and Carnap, condones the use of bound variables to refer to abstract entities known and unknown, specifiable and unspecifiable, indiscriminately.

Conceptualism holds that there are universals but they are mind-made. *Intuitionism,* espoused in modern times in one form or another by Poincaré, Brouwer, Weyl, and others, countenances the use of bound variables to refer to abstract entities only when those entities are capable of being cooked up individually from ingredients specified in advance. As Fraenkel has put it, logicism holds that classes are discovered while intuitionism holds that they are invented —a fair statement indeed of the old opposition between realism and conceptualism. This opposition is no mere quibble; it makes an essential difference in the amount of classical mathematics to which one is willing to subscribe. Logicists, or realists, are able on their assumptions to get Cantor's ascending orders of infinity; intuitionists are compelled to stop with the lowest order of infinity, and, as an indirect consequence, to abandon even some of the classical laws of real numbers. The modern controversy between logicism and intuitionism arose, in fact, from disagreements over infinity.

Formalism, associated with the name of Hilbert, echoes intuitionism in deploring the logicist's unbridled recourse to universals. But formalism also finds intuitionism unsatisfactory. This could happen for either of two opposite reasons. The formalist might, like the logicist, object to the crippling of classical mathematics; or he might, like the *nominalists* of old, object to admitting abstract entities at all, even in the restrained sense of mind-made entities. The upshot is the same: the formalist keeps classical mathematics as a play of insignificant notations. This play of notations can still be of utility—whatever utility it has already shown itself to have as a crutch for physicists and technologists. But utility need not imply significance, in any literal linguistic sense. Nor need the marked success of mathematicians in spinning out theorems, and in finding objective bases for agreement with one another's results, imply significance. For an adequate basis for agreement among mathematicians can be found simply in the rules which govern the manipulation of the notations—these syntactical rules being, unlike the notations themselves, quite significant and intelligible.

I have argued that the sort of ontology we adopt can be consequential—notably in connection with mathematics, although this is only an example. Now how are we to adjudicate among rival ontologies? Certainly the answer is not provided by the semantical formula "To be is to be the value of a variable"; this formula serves rather, conversely, in testing the conformity of a given remark or doctrine to a prior ontological standard. We look to bound variables in connection with ontology not in order to know what there is, but in order to know what a given remark or doctrine, ours or someone else's, *says* there is; and this much is quite properly a problem involving language. But what there is is another question. . . .

Our acceptance of an ontology is, I think, similar in principle to our acceptance of a scientific theory, say a system of physics: we adopt, at least insofar as we are reasonable, the simplest conceptual scheme into which the disordered fragments of raw experience can be fitted and arranged. Our ontology is determined once we have fixed upon the over-all conceptual scheme which is to accommodate science in the broadest sense; and the considerations which determine a reasonable construction of any part of that conceptual scheme, for example, the biological or the physical part, are not different in kind from the considerations which determine a reasonable construction of the whole. To whatever extent the adoption of any system of scientific theory may be said to be a matter of language, the same—but no more—may be said of the adoption of an ontology.

But simplicity, as a guiding principle in constructing conceptual schemes, is not a clear and unambiguous idea; and it is quite capable of presenting a double or multiple standard. Imagine, for example, that we have devised the most economical set of concepts adequate to the play-by-play reporting of immediate experience. The entities under this scheme—the values of bound variables—are, let us suppose, individual subjective events of sensation or reflection. We should still find, no doubt, that a physicalistic conceptual scheme, purporting to talk about external objects, offers great advantages in simplifying our over-all reports. By bringing together scattered sense events and treating them as perceptions of one object, we reduce the complexity of our stream of experience to a manageable conceptual simplicity. The rule of simplicity is indeed our guiding maxim in assigning sense data to objects: we associate an earlier and a later round sensum with the same so-called penny, or with two different so-called pennies, in obedience to the demands of maximum simplicity in our total world-picture.

Here we have two competing conceptual schemes, a phenomenalistic one and a physicalistic one. Which should prevail? Each has its advantages; each has its special simplicity in its own way. Each, I suggest, deserves to be developed. Each may be said, indeed, to be the more fundamental, though in different senses: the one is epistemologically, the other physically, fundamental.

The physical conceptual scheme simplifies our account of experience because of the way myriad scattered sense events come to be associated with single so-called objects; still there is no likelihood that each sentence about physical objects can actually be translated, however deviously and complexly, into the phenomenalistic language. Physical objects are postulated entities which round out and simplify our account of the flux of experience, just as the introduction of irrational numbers simplifies laws of arithmetic. From the point of view of the conceptual scheme of the elementary arithmetic of rational numbers alone, the broader arithmetic of rational and irrational numbers would have the status of a convenient myth, simpler than the literal truth (namely, the arithmetic of rationals) and yet containing that literal truth as a scattered part. Similarly, from a phenomenalistic point of view, the conceptual scheme of physical objects is a convenient myth, simpler than the literal truth and yet containing that literal truth as a scattered part.

Now what of classes or attributes of physical objects, in turn? A platonistic ontology of this sort is, from the point of view of a strictly physicalistic conceptual scheme, as much a myth as that physicalistic conceptual scheme itself is for phenomenalism. This higher myth is a good and useful one, in turn, in so far as it simplifies our account of physics. Since mathematics is an integral part of this higher myth, the utility of this myth for physical science is evident enough. In speaking of it nevertheless as a myth, I echo that philosophy of mathematics to which I alluded earlier under the name of formalism. But an attitude of formalism may with equal justice be adopted toward the physical conceptual scheme, in turn, by the pure aesthete or phenomenalist.

J . RENFORD BAMBROUGH

Universals and Family Resemblances

J. Renford Bambrough, (1926–   ) Tutor and Lecturer of St. John's College, Cambridge, attempts in this paper to mediate between the positions of nominalists and realists about universals.

If I ask you what these three books have in common, or what those four chairs have in common, you will look to see if the books are all on the same subject or by the same author or published by the same firm; to see if the chairs are all Chippendale or all three-legged or all marked "Not to be removed from this room." It will never occur to you to say that the books have in common that they are books or the chairs that they are chairs. And if you find after close inspection that the chairs or the books do not have in common any of the features I have mentioned, and if you cannot see any other specific feature that they have in common, you will say that as far as you can see they have nothing in common. You will perhaps add that you suppose from the form of my question that I must know of something that they have in common. I may then tell you that all the books once belonged to John Locke or that all the chairs came from Ten Rillington Place. But it would be a poor sort of joke for me to say that the chairs were all chairs or that the books were all books.

If I ask you what *all* chairs have in common, or what *all* books have in common, you may again try to find a feature like those you would look for in the case of *these three* books or *those four* chairs; and you may again think that it is a poor sort of joke for me to say that what all books have in common is that they are books and that what all chairs have in common is that they are chairs. And yet this time it is not a joke but an important philosophical truth.

Because the normal case where we ask "What have all *these* chairs, books or games in common?" is one in which we are not concerned with their all being chairs, books or games, we are liable to overlook the extreme peculiarity of the *philosophical* question that is asked with the words "What do *all* chairs, *all* books, *all*

From J. Renford Bambrough, "Universals and Family Resemblances," *Proceedings of the Aristotelian Soc. N. S.,* **61**, pp. 215–222. © The Aristotelian Society, 1961. Reprinted by courtesy of the Editor of the Aristotelian Society.

games have in common?" For of course games *do* have something in common. They *must* have something in common, and yet when we look for what they have in common we cannot find it. When we try to say what they have in common we always fail. And this is not because what we are looking for lies deeply hidden, but because it is too obvious to be seen; not because what we are trying to say is too subtle and complicated to be said, but because it is too easy and too simple to be worth saying: and so we say something more dramatic, but something false, instead. The simple truth is that what games have in common is that they are games. The nominalist is obscurely aware of this, and by rejecting the realist's talk of transcendent, immanent or subsistent forms or universals he shows his awareness. But by his own insistence that games have nothing in common except that they are called games he shows the obscurity of his awareness. The realist too is obscurely aware of it. By his talk of transcendent, immanent or subsistent forms or universals he shows the obscurity of his awareness. But by his hostility to the nominalist's insistence that games have nothing in common except that they are called games he shows his awareness.

All this can be more fully explained by the application of what I will call "Ramsey's Maxim." F. P. Ramsey, after mapping the course of an inconclusive dispute between Russell and W. E. Johnson, writes as follows:

> Evidently, however, none of these arguments are really decisive, and the position is extremely unsatisfactory to any one with real curiosity about such a fundamental question. In such cases it is a heuristic maxim that the truth lies not in one of the two disputed views but in some third possibility which has not yet been thought of, which we can only discover by rejecting something assumed as obvious by both the disputants. (*The Foundations of Mathematics*, pp. 115–116.)

It is assumed as obvious by both the nominalist and the realist that there can be no objective justification for the application of a general term to its instances unless its instances have something in common over and above their having in common that they *are* its instances. The nominalist rightly holds that there is no such additional common element, and he therefore wrongly concludes that there is no objective justification for the application of any general term. The realist rightly holds that there is an objective justification for the application of general terms, and he therefore wrongly concludes that there *must* be some additional common element.

Wittgenstein [1] denied the assumption that is common to nominalism and realism, and that is why I say that he solved the problem of universals. For if we deny the mistaken premiss that is common to the realist's argument and the nominalist's argument then we can deny the realist's mistaken conclusion and deny the nominalist's mistaken conclusion; and that is another way of saying that we can affirm the true premiss of the nominalist's argument and can also affirm the true premiss of the realist's argument.

The nominalist says that games have nothing in common except that they are called games.

The realist says that games must have something in common, and he means by this that they must have something in common other than that they are games.

Wittgenstein says that games have nothing in common except that they are games.

Wittgenstein thus denies at one and the same time the nominalist's claim that games have nothing in common except that they are called games and the realist's claim that games have something in common other than that they are games. He asserts at one and the same time the realist's claim that there is an objective justification for the application of the word "game" to games and the nominalist's claim that there is no element that is common to all games. And he is able to do all this because he denies the joint claim of the nominalist and the realist that there cannot be an objective justification for the application of the word "game" to games unless there is an element that is common to all games (*universalia in rebus*) or a common relation that all games bear to something that is not a game (*universalia ante res*).

Wittgenstein is easily confused with the nominalist because he denies what the realist asserts: that games have something in common other than that they are games.

When we see that Wittgenstein is not a nominalist we may easily confuse him with the realist because he denies what the nominalist asserts: that games have nothing in common except that they are called games.

But we can now see that Wittgenstein is neither a realist nor a nominalist: he asserts the simple truth that they both deny and he

[1] Ludwig Wittgenstein (1889–1951), an Austrian-born philosopher who worked in Cambridge. Wittgenstein has had a profound effect on English and American philosophy, being the most original of the "analytic" or "linguistic" philosophers.—Ed.

also asserts the two simple truths of which each of them asserts one and denies the other.

I will now try to put some flesh on to these bare bones.

The value and the limitations of the nominalist's claim that things which are called by the same name have nothing in common except that they are called by the same name can be seen if we look at a case where a set of objects literally and undeniably have nothing in common except that they are called by the same name. If I choose to give the name "alpha" to each of a number of miscellaneous objects (the star Sirius, my fountain-pen, the Parthenon, the colour red, the number five, and the letter Z) then I may well succeed in choosing the objects so *arbitrarily* that I shall succeed in preventing them from having any feature in common, other than that I call them by the name "alpha." But this imaginary case, to which the nominalist likens the use of all general words, has only to be described to be sharply contrasted with the typical case in which I apply a general word, say "chair", to a number of the instances to which it applies. In the first place, the *arbitrariness* of my selection of alphas is not paralleled in the case in which I apply the word "chair" successively to the chair in which I am now sitting, the Speaker's Chair in the House of Commons, the chair used at Bisley for carrying the winner of the Queen's Prize, and one of the deck chairs on the beach at Brighton. In giving a list of chairs I cannot just mention anything that happens to come into my head, while this is exactly what I do in giving my list of alphas. The second point is that the class of alphas is a *closed* class. Once I have given my list I have referred to every single alpha in the universe, actual and possible. Although I *might* have included or excluded any actual or possible object whatsoever when I was drawing up my list, once I have in fact made my arbitrary choice, no further application can be given to the word "alpha" according to the use that I have prescribed. For if I later add an object that I excluded from my list, or remove an object that I included in it, then I am making a different use of the word "alpha." With the word "chair" the position is quite different. There are an infinite number of actual and possible chairs. I cannot aspire to complete the enumeration of all chairs, as I can arbitrarily and at any point complete the enumeration of all alphas, and the word "chair," unlike the word "alpha", can be applied to an infinite number of instances without suffering any change of use.

These two points lead to a third and decisive point. I cannot teach the use of the word "alpha" except by specifically attaching it to each of the objects in my arbitrarily chosen list. No observer can conclude anything from watching me attach the label to this, that, or the other object, or to any number of objects however large, about the nature of the object or objects, if any, to which I shall later attach it. The use of the word "alpha" cannot be learned or taught as the use of a general word can be learned or taught. In teaching the use of a general word we may and must refer to characteristics of the objects to which it applies, and of the objects to which it does not apply, and indicate which of these characteristics count for the application of the word and which count against it. A pupil does not have to consult us on every separate occasion on which he encounters a new object, and if he did consult us every time we should have to say that he was not *learning* the use of the word. The reference that we make to a finite number of objects to which the word applies, and to a finite number of objects to which the word does not apply, is capable of equipping the pupil with a capacity for correctly applying or withholding the word to or from an infinite number of objects to which we have made no reference.

All this remains true in the case where it is not I alone, but a large number of people, or all of us, who use the word "alpha" in the way that I suggest. Even if everybody always called a particular set of objects by the same name, that would be insufficient to ensure that the name was a general name, and the claim of the name to be a general name would be defeated by just that necessity for reference to the arbitrary choices of the users of the name that the nominalist mistakenly claims to find in the case of a genuinely general name. For the nominalist is right in thinking that if we always had to make such a reference then there would be no general names as they are understood by the realist.

The nominalist is also right in the stress that he puts on the role of human interests and human purposes in determining our choice of principles of classification. How this insistence on the rôle of human purposes may be reconciled with the realist's proper insistence on the objectivity of the similarities and dissimilarities on which any genuine classification is based can be seen by considering an imaginary tribe of South Sea Islanders.

Let us suppose that trees are of great importance in the life and work of the South Sea Islanders, and that they have a rich and highly developed language in which they speak of the trees with which their island is thickly clad. But they do not have names for the species and genera of trees as they are recognised by our botanists. As we walk round the island with some of its inhabitants we can easily pick out orange-trees, date-palms and cedars. Our hosts are puzzled that we should call by the same name trees which appear to them to have nothing in common. They in turn surprise us by giving the same name to each of the trees in what is from our point of view a very mixed plantation. They point out to us what they called a mixed plantation and we see that it is in our terms a clump of trees of the same species. Each party comes to recognise that its own classifications are as puzzling to the other as the other's are puzzling to itself.

This looks like the sort of situation that gives aid and comfort to the nominalist in his battle against the realist. But if we look at it more closely we see that it cannot help him. We know already that our own classification is based on similarities and differences between the trees, similarities and differences which we can point out to the islanders in an attempt to teach them our language. Of course we may fail, but if we do it will not be because we *must* fail.

Now *either* (*a*) The islanders have means of teaching us their classifications, by pointing out similarities and differences which we had not noticed, or in which we had not been interested, in which case *both* classifications are genuine, and no rivalry between them, of a kind that can help the nominalist, could ever arise; *or* (*b*) Their classification is arbitrary in the sense in which my use of the word "alpha" was arbitrary, in which case it is not a genuine classification.

It may be that the islanders classify trees as "boat-building trees", "house-building trees," etc., and that they are more concerned with the height, thickness and maturity of the trees than they are with the distinctions of species that interest us.

In a particular case of *prima facie* conflict of classifications, we may not in fact be able to discover whether what appears to be a rival classification really *is* a classification. But we can be sure that *if* it is a classification *then* it is backed by objective similarities and differences, and that if it is *not* backed by objective similarities and differences then it is merely an arbitrary system of names. In no case will it appear that we must choose between rival systems of genuine classification of a set of objects in such a sense that one of them is to be recognised as *the* classification for all purposes.

There is no limit to the number of possible classifications of objects. (The nominalist is right about this.) [2]

There is no classification of any set of objects which is not objectively based on genuine similarities and differences. (The realist is right about this.)

The nominalist is so impressed by the infinite diversity of possible classifications that he is blinded to their objectivity.

The realist is so impressed by the objectivity of all genuine classifications that he underestimates their diversity.

Of course we may if we like say that there is one complete system of classification which marks all the similarities and all the differences. (This is the realist's summing up of what we can learn by giving critical attention to the realist and the nominalist in turn.)

Or we may say that there are only similarities and differences, from which we may choose according to our purposes and interests. (This is the nominalist's summing up.)

In talking of genuine or objective similarities and differences we must not forget that we are concerned with similarities and differences between *possible* cases as well as between actual cases, and indeed that we are concerned with the actual cases only because they are themselves a selection of the possible cases.

Because the nominalist and the realist are both right and both wrong, each is driven into the other's arms when he tries to be both consistent and faithful to our language, knowledge and experience. The nominalist talks of resemblances until he is pressed into a corner where he must acknowledge that resemblance is unintelligible except as resemblance *in a respect*, and to specify the respect in which objects resemble one another is to indicate a *quality* or *property*. The realist talks of properties and qualities until, when properties and qualities have been explained in terms of other properties and other qualities, he can at last do nothing but point to the *resemblances* between the objects that are said to be characterised by such and such a property or quality.

The question "Are resemblances ultimate or are properties ultimate?" is a perverse question if it is meant as one to which there

---

[2] Here one may think of Wittgenstein's remark that "Every application of every word is arbitrary," which emphasises that we can always find *some* distinction between any pair of objects, however closely similar they may be. What might be called the principle of the diversity of discernibles guarantees that we can never be *forced* to apply the same word to two different things.

must be a simple, *single* answer. They are both ultimate, or neither is ultimate. The craving for a single answer is the logically unsatisfiable craving for something that will be the ultimate terminus of explanation and will yet itself be explained.

A . D . W O O Z L E Y

Facts and Propositions

A. D. Woozley (1912–   ), Professor of Moral Philosophy at the University of St. Andrews, was educated at Hallebury College and at Queen's College, Oxford. His Theory of Knowledge was published in 1949. In it he makes clear many valuable distinctions such as the one between propositions and facts, quoted here.

The first question that naturally falls to be asked about the Correspondence theory is what the terms are between which the relation of correspondence holds. So far, we have interpreted the theory as saying that it is a relation between a belief, on the one hand, and the facts of the case, on the other. Is it, then, to be a relation between one fact and another, the first always being a fact involving a belief or a judgment? For that I believe the sun is shining is just as good an objective fact as the fact that the sun is shining. The answer to this question is, I think, that we may say, if we like, that the correspondence is between the fact that I believe the sun in shining and the fact that the sun is shining, but that is not a particularly helpful thing to say. It is not helpful, because it may disguise from our attention the element in the belief which is of primary relevance to the Correspondence theory [1]—namely, *what* I believe. If correspondence is a relation between belief and fact, then that *I* believe that the sun is shining rather than that *you* believe it seems unimportant: which of us happens to hold the belief will not alter the relation of correspondence between belief and fact.

Again, it does not matter whether what I have so far called 'belief' is more determinately specified as 'settled conviction' or

From A. D. Woozley, *Theory of Knowledge* (London: Hutchinson University Library, 1949), pp. 134–137. Used by permission of Hutchinson & Co. (Publishers) Ltd., London.

[1] Woozley's discussion of the nature of propositions and facts occurs in connection with his account of the Correspondence theory as to the nature of truth. On this theory an empirical statement is true if the proposition or meaning asserted by the statement corresponds to an objective fact of the real world. Thus the proposition expressed by the sentence, "It is raining here now" is true if and only if it is a fact that rain is falling here now.—Ed.

'wavering opinion,' or just plain 'hunch': what sort of a believing it is makes no difference to whether the belief is true or not. Therefore, although it would on the Correspondence theory be in a perfectly good sense true that correspondence would be a relation between two facts, it would nevertheless be misleading so to describe it. The correspondence will be between what is believed and the fact of the sun shining; and following the procedure laid down in the last chapter, we may refer to what is believed by calling it a proposition.

That does not require us to hold that there are mysterious things, perceptible only to philosophers, called propositions; all it does is to call attention to the fact that whenever we believe we believe something, and that when we speak or write our sentences have (normally) a meaning. As the proposition that the sun is shining is that part of my belief that the sun is shining in virtue of which my belief (or the fact of it) could be said to correspond to the fact of the sun shining, I propose hereafter, in discussing the Correspondence theory, to speak of a proposition as being one term of the relation, as being that which is wanted to correspond with whatever makes the belief in question true. This, I think, is the normal procedure of Correspondence supporters, and it is also, I suspect, where they go wrong; but discussion of this suspicion must be deferred until the next chapter.

What of the other term, that in virtue of which a proposition is true? So far, it has been referred to as a fact, but that it is a fact has not yet been defended, nor, indeed, has fact been defined. Although I do not think "fact" can be defined, yet what philosophers might call "a definition in use" can perhaps be given, i.e. enough can be said about it to recognize what we are referring to when we refer to something as a fact; and it can best be indicated by contrasting it with an event. To say of *x* that it was an event is to say that it was a temporal occurrence. How long it lasts is quite unimportant, and whether we regard a temporal slice of history or a process as one event or as a sequence of events is purely conventional. We may equally say of an athletics meeting that it was the chief sporting event of the season, and of the hundred yards race at that meeting that it was the first event on the programme. . . .

The dropping of the atom bomb on Hiroshima was an event which occurred in August 1945; there is a fact that an atom bomb was dropped on Hiroshima in August 1945, but the fact did not occur then. We use the various tenses (past, present, and future) of verbs to indicate the occurrence of events, but only the non-temporal present indicative of the verb 'to be' to indicate facts.[2] A fact in this respect is, as it were, an hypostasized event, an abstraction of what happened in an event. The actual event of the dropping of the bomb on Hiroshima was an enormously complicated occurrence, far too complicated to describe in even approximate detail; the fact is a conveniently intelligible aspect of the event, the way an event looks to a mind thinking about it.

Again, according to ordinary usage, an event is singular, which a fact need not be. The fact that an atom bomb was dropped on Hiroshima in August 1945 is singular in that it refers to what happened at a particular place on a particular date; and if no bomb had been dropped on that place on that date there would be no such fact. But we also speak of general facts, such as natural laws of greater or narrower range. A man may be unaware of the fact that in England we drive on the left-hand side of the road; it is a commonly accepted fact that in a free economy increase in purchasing power is followed by increase in prices; no scientist will dispute the fact that water expands when it freezes; and so on. By saying that these are facts we are not referring to any particular event. Even though we may be referring to a *class* of events, it might be a class with no members. Scientists might have discovered the natural laws about the expansion of water, even though no water had ever frozen, and they certainly make use of laws about frictionless engines, even though no such engine has been, or will in the present causal system, be built.

We may further speak of universal and necessary facts, which are contrasted with those expressed in natural laws, because although the latter could conceivably have been different from what they are, the former could not. Although it is not the case that heated metals contract, it is conceivable that they should; we should be surprised, and maybe indignant, to discover to-morrow that they do, but we cannot know *a priori* that they will not. On the other hand that $2 + 3 = 5$, that if $A > B$ and $B > C$, then $A > C$, that whatever is coloured is extended are held to be necessary facts,

---

[2] An apparent exception, e.g. "The fact that an atom bomb was dropped on Hiroshima accelerated the Japanese government's surrender" is only apparent. For it was not that fact which accelerated the surrender, but the Japanese rulers' realization of it; and that realization was itself an event or a complex of events.

which would apply not only in this, but in any other conceivable world.

That explanation should suffice to show in what sense I am using 'facts,' the sense in which, so far as I know, it is commonly used. . . .

PART III

The Nature of Metaphysical Knowledge

CLARENCE I. LEWIS

Metaphysical Meaning

Clarence I. Lewis (1883–1964), long-time professor at Harvard, distinguished logician and epistemologist, is especially well known for his book, Mind and the World-Order, *and for his Carus lectures,* An Analysis of Knowledge and Valuation. *In his Presidential address to the American Philosophical Association on "Experience and Meaning," reprinted here in part, he goes far toward a definitive account of empirical meaningfulness.*

One may be tempted, in protest against various forms of transcendentalism and verbalism, to announce the unqualified dictum that only what is verifiable can be known, and only what is knowable can be the subject of a meaningful hypothesis. But such flat statement, while true in general, may nevertheless be misleading on account of an ambiguity in the word 'verifiable'. On the one hand this connotes a certain character of the content of one's assertion or hypothesis. This must be envisaged in sensuous terms; it must be the case that we could recognize certain empirical eventualities as verifying it, supposing that the conditions of such verifying experience could be satisfied. Verifiability in this sense requires an empirical *content* of the hypothesis, but has nothing to do with the practical or even the theoretical difficulties of verification. Whatever further restrictions may be appropriate in physics or any other nat-

From Clarence I. Lewis, "Experience and Meaning," *The Philosophical Review,* **XLIII** (1934), 140–145. Reprinted by permission of the author and the editor of *The Philosophical Review.*

ural science, the only general requirement of empirical meaning—which alone is pertinent to those hypotheses about reality which philosophy must consider—is this limitation to what can be expressed in terms which genuinely possess denotation.

On the other hand, 'verifiable' connotes the possibility of actually satisfying the conditions of verification. Or, to put it otherwise, verifiability may be taken to require 'possible experience' *as conditioned by the actual;* we must be able to find our way, step by step, from where we actually stand to this verifying experience. Hence practical or theoretical difficulties are limitations of verifiability in this second sense. These limitations may be genuinely pertinent to knowledge, because *knowledge* requires the *assurance of truth;* and whatever would prevent actual verification may prevent such assurance. But verifiability in this second sense has no relevance to meaning, because the assurance of truth is, obviously, not a condition of meaningfulness.

It is of importance to avoid confusing these two senses of 'verifiable' in assessing the significance of those considerations which methodological solipsism makes prominent. If it could be said that actual knowing must rest upon verification which, in the end, must be first-person and must be here and now when the knowing occurs, at least it would be an absurdity to translate this into the negation of meaning to whatever cannot be expressed in terms of first-person experience and of experience here and now. I impute this absurdity to no one; I would merely urge the necessity of avoiding it. . . .

One traditional problem of metaphysics is immortality. The hypothesis of immortality is unverifiable in an obvious sense. Yet it is an hypothesis about our own future experience. And our understanding of what would verify it has no lack of clarity. It may well be that, apart from a supposed connection with more exigent and mundane problems such as those of ethics, this hypothesis is not a fruitful topic of philosophic consideration. But if it be maintained that only what is scientifically verifiable has meaning, then this conception is a case in point. It could hardly be verified by science; and there is no observation or experiment which science could make, the negative result of which would disprove it. That consideration, however, has nothing to do with its meaningfulness as an hypothesis about reality. To deny that this conception has an empirical content would be as little justified as to deny empirical content to the belief that these hills will still be here when we are gone.

Next let us consider that question about the external world, supposedly at issue between idealists and realists. One suspects that the real animus of debate between these two parties is, and always has been, a concern with the question of an essential relationship between cosmic processes and human values; and that if, historically, idealists have sought to capture their conclusion on this point by arguments derived from a Berkeleyan or similar analysis of knowledge, at least such attempt has been abandoned in current discussion. So that this question about the external world, in any easily statable form, is probably not pertinent to present controversy. But there is one formulation which, if it is too naïve to be thus pertinent, at least poses an intelligible question about the nature of reality. Let us phrase this as a realistic hypothesis: If all minds should disappear from the universe, the stars would still go on in their courses.

This hypothesis is humanly unverifiable. That, however, is merely a predicament, which prevents assurance of truth but does not affect meaning. We can only express or envisage this hypothesis by means of imagination, and hence in terms of what any mind like ours *would* experience if, contrary to hypothesis, any mind *should* be there. But we do not need to commit the Berkeleyan naïveté of arguing that it is impossible to imagine a tree on a desert island which nobody is thinking of—because we are thinking of it ourselves. It is entirely meaningful, for example, to think of those inventions which nobody has ever thought of, or those numbers which no one will ever count; we can even frame the concept of those concepts which no one will ever frame. Those who would deny this on logical grounds exhibit a sense of paradox of language which is stronger than their sense of fact. Furthermore, *imagination* is sufficient for empirical meaning, though it requires *perception* for verification. I can imagine that future time which I shall never perceive; and humans can meaningfully think of that future when humanity may have run its cosmic course and all consciousness will have disappeared. It may be that the hypothesis of a reality with no sentience to be affected by it is not a particularly significant issue; though the idealist might have an interest in it for the sake of the light which decision about it would throw upon the nature which reality has now. In any case, the fact that it is unverifiable has no bearing upon its meaningfulness. Whether this hypothesis is true, is a genuine question about the nature of reality.

Finally, we may turn to the conception of other selves. The importance which this topic has for ethics will be obvious. Descartes conceived that the lower animals are a kind of automata; and the monstrous supposition that other humans are merely robots would have meaning if there should ever be a consistent solipsist to make it. The logical positivist does not deny that other humans have feelings; he circumvents the issue by a behavioristic interpretation of "having feelings". He points out that your toothache is a verifiable object of my knowledge; it is a construction put upon certain empirical items which are data for me—your tooth and your behavior. My own toothache is equally a construction. Until there are such prior constructions as the physical concept "teeth", from given sense-data, neither your toothache nor mine is a possible object of knowledge. And, similarly, until there is a construction involving such prior constructions as human bodies, there is no own-self or yourself as particular objects of knowledge. As knowable things, myself and yourself are equally constructions; and though as constructed objects they are fundamentally different in kind, the constructions are coördinate. That experience which is the original datum of *all* such constructions is, in Carnap's phrase, "without a subject." [1] Nevertheless it has that quality or status, characteristic of all given experience, which is indicated by the adjective "first-person".

With the general manner of this account of our knowledge of ourselves and others I think we should agree. But it does not touch the point at issue. Suppose I fear that I may have a toothache tomorrow. I entertain a conception involving various constructions from present data; my body, teeth, etc. But my present experience, by which I know or anticipate this future toothache, is not an experience of an *ache*. There is here that difference which has been noted between the experience which entertains and the experience which would verify, to which it implicitly refers. A robot could have a toothache, in the sense of having a swollen jaw and exhibiting all the appropriate behavior; but there would be no pain connected with it. The question of metaphysical solipsism is the question whether there is any pain connected with your observed behavior indicating toothache. The logical positivist claims that this issue has no meaning, because there is no empirical content which could verify the non-solipsistic assertion—that is, no content unless, following his procedure, I identify your pain with observable items such as the behavior which exhibits it; in which case it is verifiable in the

[1] See *Der Logische Aufbau der Welt*, § 65.

first person. To make this identification, however, is to beg precisely the point at issue.

Let us compare the two cases of your toothache now and my toothache tomorrow. I cannot verify your toothache, as distinct from your observable behavior, because of the egocentric predicament. But neither can I verify my own future toothache—because of the now-predicament. My tomorrow's pain, however, may genuinely be an object of knowledge for me now, because a pain may be cognized by an experience in which that pain is not a given ingredient. (The imagination of a pain may be painful; but it is not the pain anticipated. If it were, all future events which we anticipate would be happening already.) *Your* pain I can *never* verify. But when I assert that you are not an automaton, I can envisage what I mean—and what makes the difference between the truth and falsity of my assertion—because I can imagine your pain, as distinct from all I can literally experience of you, just as I can imagine my own future pain, as distinct from the experience in which I now imagine it.

In the nature of the case I cannot verify you as another center of experience distinct from myself. Any verification which I might suppose myself to make would violate the hypothesis by being first-person experience. But there is nothing to which I can give more explicit empirical content than the supposition of a consciousness like mine connected with a body like my own. Whether there is any such would be a terribly important question about reality if anybody entertained a doubt about the answer. Whether you are another mind or only a sleep-walking body is a question of fact. And it cannot be exorcized by definitions—by defining 'meaningful' so as to limit it to the verifiable, and 'verifiable' by reference to the egocentric predicament.

This conception of other selves as metaphysical ultimates exemplifies the philosophic importance which may attach to a supposition which is nevertheless unverifiable on account of the limitations of knowing. Though empirical meaning is requisite to theoretical significance—and that consideration is of first importance in guarding against verbal nonsense in philosophy—still the sense in which a supposition is meaningful often outruns that in which the assurance of truth, by verification, can genuinely be hoped for. In limiting cases like this last question it may even outrun the possibility of verification altogether.

IMMANUEL KANT

The Peculiarity of
Metaphysical Judgments

Immanuel Kant (1724–1804) is widely regarded as one of the world's great philosophers. His most famous work, The Critique of Pure Reason, *is difficult reading, but his* Prolegomena, *excerpted here, is more readily followed. He distinguishes a priori from a posteriori judgments, and analytic from synthetic ones. Metaphysical judgments are, according to him, both a priori and synthetic.*

As concerns the sources of metaphysical knowledge, its very concept implies that they cannot be empirical. Its principles (including not only its maxims but its basic notions) must never be derived from experience. It must not be physical but metaphysical knowledge, namely, knowledge lying beyond experience. It can therefore have for its basis neither external experience, which is the source of physics proper, nor internal, which is the basis of empirical psychology. It is therefore *a priori* knowledge, coming from pure understanding and pure reason.

But so far metaphysics would not be distinguishable from pure mathematics; it must therefore be called *pure philosophical* knowledge; and for the meaning of this term I refer to the *Critique of Pure Reason*,[1] where the distinction between these two employments of reason is sufficiently explained. So far concerning the sources of metaphysical knowledge.

a. On the Distinction between Analytical and Synthetical Judgments in General.—The peculiarity of its sources demands that metaphysical knowledge must consist of nothing but *a priori* judgments. But whatever be their origin or their logical form, there is a distinction in judgments, as to their content, according to which they are either merely *explicative*, adding nothing to the content of knowledge, or *expansive*, increasing the given knowledge. The former may be called *analytical*, the latter *synthetical*, judgments.

From Immanuel Kant, *Prolegomena to Any Future Metaphysics*, trans. Lewis W. Beck, copyright 1951 by The Liberal Arts Press, Inc., pp. 13–19 *passim.*, and reprinted by permission of the Liberal Arts Press Division of The Bobbs-Merrill Company, Inc.

[1] *Critique of Pure Reason*, "Methodology," Ch. I, Sec. 2.

Analytical judgments express nothing in the predicate but what has been already actually thought in the concept of the subject, though not so distinctly or with the same (full) consciousness. When I say: "All bodies are extended," I have not amplified in the least my concept of body, but have only analyzed it, as extension was really thought to belong to that concept before the judgment was made, though it was not expressed. This judgment is therefore analytical. On the contrary, this judgment, "Some bodies have weight," contains in its predicate something not actually thought in the universal concept of body; it amplifies my knowledge by adding something to my concept, and must therefore be called synthetical.

b. The Common Principle of All Analytical Judgments Is the Law of Contradiction.—All analytical judgments depend wholly on the law of contradiction, and are in their nature *a priori* cognitions, whether the concepts that supply them with matter be empirical or not. For the predicate of an affirmative analytical judgment is already contained in the concept of the subject, of which it cannot be denied without contradiction. In the same way its opposite is necessarily denied of the subject in an analytical, but negative, judgment, by the same law of contradiction. Such is the nature of the judgments: "All bodies are extended," and "No bodies are unextended (that is, simple)."

For this very reason all analytical judgments are *a priori* even when the concepts are empirical, as, for example, "Gold is a yellow metal"; for to know this I require no experience beyond my concept of gold as a yellow metal. It is, in fact, the very concept, and I need only analyze it without looking beyond it.

c. Synthetical Judgments Require A Different Principle from the Law of Contradiction.—There are synthetical *a posteriori* judgments of empirical origin; but there are also others which are certain *a priori*, and which spring from pure understanding and reason. Yet they both agree in this, that they cannot possibly spring from the principle of analysis, namely, the law of contradiction, alone. They require a quite different principle from which they may be deduced, subject, of course, always to the law of contradiction, which must never be violated, even though everything cannot be deduced from it. I shall first classify synthetical judgments.

1. *Judgments of Experience* are always synthetical. For it would be absurd to base an analytical judgment on experience, as our concept suffices for the purpose without requiring any testimony from experience. That body is extended is a judgment established

a priori, and not an empirical judgment. For before appealing to experience, we already have all the conditions of the judgment in the concept, from which we have but to elicit the predicate according to the law of contradiction, and thereby to become conscious of the necessity of the judgment, which experience could not in the least teach us.

2. *Mathematical Judgments* are all synthetical. . . .

First of all, we must observe that all strictly mathematical judgments are *a priori,* and not empirical, because they carry with them necessity, which cannot be obtained from experience. But if this be not conceded to me, very good; I shall confine my assertion to *pure mathematics,* the very notion of which implies that it contains pure *a priori* and not empirical knowledge.

It must at first be thought that the proposition $7 + 5 = 12$ is a mere analytical judgment, following from the concept of the sum of seven and five, according to the law of contradiction. But on closer examination it appears that the concept of the sum of $7 + 5$ contains merely their union in a single number, without its being at all thought what the particular number is that unites them. The concept of twelve is by no means thought by merely thinking of the combination of seven and five; and, analyze this possible sum as we may, we shall not discover twelve in the concept. We must go beyond these concepts, by calling to our aid some intuition which corresponds to one of the concepts—that is, either our five fingers or five points (as Segner has it in his *Arithmetic*)—and we must add successively the units of the five given in the intuition of the concept of seven. Hence our concept is really amplified by the proposition $7 + 5 = 12$, and we add to the first concept a second concept not thought in it. Arithmetical judgments are therefore synthetical, and the more plainly according as we take larger numbers; for in such cases it is clear that, however closely we analyze our concepts without calling intuition to our aid, we can never find the sum by such mere dissection. . . .

The essential and distinguishing feature of pure mathematical knowledge among all other *a priori* knowledge is that it cannot at all proceed from concepts, but only by means of the construction of concepts.[2] As therefore in its propositions it must proceed beyond the concept to that which its corresponding intuition contains, these propositions neither can, nor ought to, arise analytically, by dissection of the concept, but are all synthetical. . . .

[2] *Critique of Pure Reason,* Ch. I, Sec. 1.

3. *Metaphysical Judgments*, properly so called, are all synthetical. We must distinguish judgments pertaining to metaphysics from metaphysical judgments properly so called. Many of the former are analytical, but they only afford the means for metaphysical judgments, which are the whole end of the science and which are always synthetical. For if there be concepts pertaining to metaphysics (as, for example, that of substance), the judgments springing from simple analysis of them also pertain to metaphysics, as, for example, substance is that which only exists as subject, etc.; and by means of several such analytical judgments we seek to approach the definition of the concepts. But as the analysis of a pure concept of the understanding (the kind of concept pertaining to metaphysics) does not proceed in any different manner from the dissection of any other, even empirical, concepts, not belonging to metaphysics (such as, air is an elastic fluid, the elasticity of which is not destroyed by any known degree of cold), it follows that the concept indeed, but not the analytical judgment, is properly metaphysical. This science has something peculiar in the production of its *a priori* cognitions, which must therefore be distinguished from the features it has in common with other rational knowledge. Thus the judgment that all the substance in things is permanent is a synthetical and properly metaphysical judgment.

If the *a priori* concepts which constitute the materials and tools of metaphysics have first been collected according to fixed principles, then their analysis will be of great value; it might be taught as a particular part (as a *philosophia definitiva*), containing nothing but analytical judgments pertaining to metaphysics, and could be treated separately from the synthetical which constitute metaphysics proper. For indeed these analyses are not of much value except in metaphysics, that is, as regards the synthetical judgments which are to be generated by these previously analyzed concepts.

The conclusion drawn in this section then is that metaphysics is properly concerned with synthetical propositions *a priori*, and these alone constitute its end, for which it indeed requires various dissections of its concepts, namely, analytical judgments, but wherein the procedure is not different from that in every other kind of knowledge, in which we merely seek to render our concepts distinct by analysis. But the generation of *a priori* knowledge by intuition as well as by concepts, in fine, of synthetical propositions *a priori*, especially in philosophical knowledge, constitutes the essential subject of metaphysics.

BERNARD A. O. WILLIAMS

Metaphysical Arguments

Bernard A. O. Williams (1929–   ) Professor of Philosophy at Bedford College in the University of London, offers in the following selection a lively and informative account of the nature of metaphysical arguments.

Metaphysicians do not just assert their positions. They attempt to support them by argument, and to give proofs of their conclusions. Some consideration of these proofs must form part of any enquiry into the nature of metaphysics; for it is the attempt to give a proof for his conclusion, to show by logical argument that such-and-such must be so, that chiefly distinguishes the philosophical metaphysican from the mystic, the moralist and others who express or try to express a comprehensive view of how things are or ought to be.

It may well be that the thorough-going metaphysician does not often, psychologically speaking, start with his proofs; he may start rather with a view of the world, and find subsequently demonstrations that articulate his thoughts in the required shape. In this sense, the arguments that he gives may be described as rationalizations—so long as this description does not mean that the arguments are therefore summarily to be dismissed as baseless, invalid or contemptible. Part of the word 'rationalization' is after all the word 'rational', and it is in virtue of their logical structure, their claims to logical validity, that metaphysical theories are marked off from mere intuitive and unformulated insights into reality.

However, the resemblance of metaphysical theories to rationalizations in the psychoanalytical sense does go rather deeper than this, and it may make one wonder whether the arguments that the metaphysician produces really *matter*. To some recent writers, metaphysical theories and arguments have seemed to be just symptoms of a kind of intellectual neurosis or 'mental cramp' [1]—the metaphysician is a man with an *idée fixe* which he projects on the world

From Bernard A. O. Williams, "Metaphysical Arguments," in D. F. Pears (ed.), *The Nature of Metaphysics* (London: Macmillan & Co. Ltd., 1957), pp. 39–60. Used by permission of Macmillan, London, and St Martin's Press, Inc., New York.

[1] This phrase, and the underlying idea, come from Wittgenstein. The most thorough-going exponent of the theory is John Wisdom—see his collection of articles, *Philosophy and Psychoanalysis,* published by Blackwell.

in the form of an ambitious and distorted theory. So, just as it is no good reasoning with a neurotic, it is no good arguing with a metaphysician—what one must do, in both cases, is to cure them. Hence there goes with this view of metaphysics a corresponding view of the proper duty of philosophy. The philosopher should play psychoanalyst to the tortured and theory-ridden metaphysician and, by-passing the arguments in which he rationalizes his worries, use analytic technique to get to the roots of the worries themselves.

In its extremer forms, this view seems to be a wild exaggeration. What it rightly emphasizes is that many important metaphysical arguments are not the sort of arguments that can just be accepted as valid or rejected as invalid by certain and generally agreed rules, and that their value or their faults are likely to lie deeper, in some central concept or idea which the metaphysician is trying to articulate through them. . . .

Of course, metaphysicians vary in the extent to which they try to give proofs of what they say; and in the extent to which the proofs that are given are precisely and rigorously expressed; and in the extent to which the proofs, however expressed, form an essential part of the thought, and are not just there for decoration. To take two comparable British metaphysicians, for instance, there is a marked difference between McTaggart and Bradley: while McTaggart seeks knock-down forms of proof and hard coal-like knobs of argument, Bradley tentatively adumbrates. Yet allowing for all these differences, there is in practically any Western metaphysician of importance a core of argument, an attempt to support his position or raise his questions by a movement from premisses to conclusion. [Logicians usually classify such arguments as either inductive or deductive.] Deductive inferences are such that if you accept the premisses, you must accept the conclusion, or else contradict yourself —the conclusion follows with rigorous logical necessity from what implies it. Such are the arguments, for instance, of mathematicians. Inductive arguments, on the other hand, have no such absolute rigour; one who accepted the premisses would not *contradict* himself if he refused to accept the conclusion, although he might look pretty silly. Most practical inferences of everyday life are of this type: thus if a man arrives from personal experience at the conclusion that it is always unwise to play cards with strangers on race trains, he is making an inductive step. . . . An inductive inference is empirical, and it is always conceivable that its conclusion should turn out to be untrue, however carefully it has been considered.

In the case of deductive arguments the situation is more complicated. Deductive arguments can have conclusions that are necessary and certain—such are the conclusions of mathematical arguments. But they will be so only if the premisses are certain as well, just because a deductive argument gives you no more in the conclusion than what is already tied up or implied in the premisses. If the premisses are only probable, then so will the conclusion be. The immediate point for the present discussion, however, is that inductive arguments can lead only to empirical and probable results.

What is the relation of metaphysical arguments to these two sorts of argument? An enquiry into this relation should at least help us to see what a metaphysical argument is not, and may help us to see something of what it is. It is clear, first, that metaphysicians do not characteristically make straightforward inductive inferences: they do not say things of the form 'such and such is true in these instances, so it is probably always true'. It would be absurd, for instance, to suppose that a metaphysician would reach the conclusion 'men have freewill' by an argument like 'all men we have observed have freewill, so men in general do' as one might argue 'all the men we have observed have eyebrows, so men in general do'. The *a priori* quality of a metaphysical conclusion, its necessity, by itself makes such a procedure inappropriate: there could be no need of *that* kind of support from experience.

Yet it must be said that some arguments that metaphysicians have employed do look remarkably like inductive inferences. Such, for example, is the simplest form of the theological argument from design, once well known under the name of 'Paley's watch'. Paley's form of it was just this: 'If we found by chance a watch or other piece of intricate mechanism we should infer that it had been made by someone. But all around us we do find intricate pieces of natural mechanism, and the processes of the universe are seen to move together in complex relations; we should therefore infer that these too have a Maker.' There are some general difficulties about an argument from analogy of this type; but the immediate point is that it does seem just to be a kind of inductive argument. Paley's reasoning is simply this: 'wherever in the past we have found intricate mechanisms we have found a maker, so in this case, too, we can infer one'. But by being an inductive argument it seems too weak for its purpose. For, taken by itself, it can lead only to an inductive type of conclusion; and so the statement of the existence of a God, to which it is supposed to lead, will have the status only of a quasi-scientific hypothesis; and for any such inductive hypothesis, as we have seen, the opposite involves no contradiction, and is logically possible. So one who from *this* type of argument accepted the existence of God would have to admit that it was at least possible that God did not exist after all. But in general one who believed in God would not admit that it was in any way possible that God did not exist; he would insist that the statement of God's existence must have some sort of absolute necessity. Thus Paley's watch, if it is to be called a metaphysical argument at all, does not seem to be a characteristic one, nor yet a characteristic argument for the existence of God. It is only, as it were, a super-scientific inference. . . .

I should like to make two points about this type of example. First, I think there certainly is, or has been, a way of doing philosophy that tried to assimilate it to the natural sciences, and hence regarded its conclusions in the light of probabilities. Some philosophers in this century, impressed by the achievements of the sciences and depressed by traditional metaphysics, sought to apply scientific methods inside philosophy itself, and the results did include what look like metaphysical conclusions presented with an air of inductive probability. I think, however, that if these arguments are closely examined, they can be found not to be straightforward inductive arguments, as Paley's perhaps was; the language of theory and probability is little more than a dressing for a philosophical conceptual argument. Moreover, these philosophers are not typical metaphysicians; they themselves, I suspect, might have denied that what they were doing was metaphysics.

Second, there may be another reason, quite different from the last, why Russell, for instance, should qualify metaphysical conclusions with terms like 'probably'. We have already seen one reason why the conclusion of an argument should be thought to be only probable: that is, just that the argument is an inductive one, and a philosopher may want to mark the empirical nature of any inductive argument by inserting 'probably' into it. If this is what Russell meant, then certainly his argument is an inductive one. But this is only one reason why the word 'probably' should occur in an argument, and there are others. Another, and very familiar, reason is that the premisses of the argument are themselves only probable, in the quite ordinary sense in which, for instance, it is (at best) only probable that the favourite will win the 2.30 at tomorrow's races. . . .

Still, there is yet another way in which 'probably' can come into an argument, and this may shed more light on Russell's. In considering an argument, we may be concerned not so much with the question of whether the premisses and the conclusion are true or false, certain or probable, as with the question of whether the conclusion follows from the premisses—that is, we may just want to know whether the argument is *valid*. Strictly speaking, there are no degrees of validity: the conclusion either follows from the premisses or it does not, and there is no middle way. It makes no sense to say that a conclusion 'more or less' or 'just about' follows. Yet one often meets the situation in which one is not *sure* whether a given argument is valid. The premisses may be complicated or unclearly expressed, the chain of reasoning subtle, and so on, and one may be in genuine doubt whether the conclusion does follow or not. In such cases, one may express one's doubts by saying that the conclusion 'perhaps' or 'probably' follows from the premisses.

This sort of doubt, and hence this sort of 'probably', can come in, of course, with any sort of argument, inductive or deductive: a piece of mathematics, for instance, may be so complicated and so little self-evident that the best one can say, pending a lot of further investigation, is that the conclusion is probably reached by valid argument. Russell's argument, and some other metaphysical arguments that involve the notion of probability, may be of this last type. The notion of probability comes into them not because the philosopher thinks that either his conclusion or his premisses are inherently dubious, but because he is doubtful about the connection between them—he is not sure whether his conclusion in fact follows. Such doubts, as we have seen, can arise with any sort of argument; and the fact that a philosopher does not commit himself to saying more than that his conclusion *perhaps* follows, does not by itself show what sort of conclusion he is reaching, or by what sort of argument.

Anyway, metaphysical arguments do not seem to be characteristically inductive. Are they then deductive?

Deduction seems a better candidate for the metaphysician's professional tool, for deductive arguments can at least lead to conclusions of necessity, which are what he wants. It is commonly said that metaphysicians seek to deduce the nature of reality or some such thing; and so the impression may be given that the metaphysician's is a wholly deductive enterprise. This impression seems to get support from the great systems that some metaphysicians have constructed, which claim to show deductive relations between features of reality.

But the idea that the metaphysical activity consists just of making deductions in a system neglects a more fundamental question. Every deductive movement must be made from one place to another: one needs both premisses and conclusion. So in a chain or system of deductions there must be something at the beginning from which the whole series of reasonings starts. In a formal logical system what one has at the beginning are axioms; these are, relative to that system, unquestionable. They are not themselves derived in the system—there is nothing to derive them from. It is possible to have a number of purely formal systems, each with its own axioms, and for particular purposes one can take one's choice. But the metaphysician is not concerned to give us a choice. He wants to make a series of statements that will both have content and be necessarily true. But if his conclusions are, as he wishes, to be inescapable, and he is deducing the conclusions ultimately from axioms, then the axioms must be inescapable as well—inferences, unlike divers, do not gain in weight as they get nearer the bottom. But the axioms cannot themselves be proved in the system; so the metaphysician must have some other method of supporting his axioms, outside the system. He will try to show that one has to accept his axioms, for only so can he show that one has to accept his conclusions. The weapon he uses to try to make one accept the axioms is in the strongest sense the metaphysical argument.

The rationalist system-builders of the seventeenth century tried in their different ways to find axioms for their systems which would be inescapable; but their method was on the whole to look for axioms which needed no support of any kind, which were self-evidently true. So their metaphysical argument at this point is rather an appeal to propositions which need no argument at all. Thus Descartes, for instance, by his procedure of systematic doubt, whittled away the truths he believed in until he arrived at the apparently indubitable truth 'I am doubting', from which he took an immediate step to 'I exist'. Whether he regarded this step as purely deductive is to me unclear; at any rate, the indubitability of 'I am doubting' seemed to him to be established by the pure light of reason.

But not all system-builders use methods as simple as this to provide their axioms. And not all metaphysicians are, in this most ambitious sense, system-builders. Our argument has shown why there is no need for them to be. For if a metaphysical argument can be used to compel one to accept a statement which is then going to be used as the axiom of a system, it can also be used to make one accept the statement even if it is not going to be used as an axiom.

Even metaphysicians not engaged in comprehensive system-building will try to show by constructive argument that such and such (which on the whole you didn't expect) must be so; or, very frequently, by destructive argument, that so and so (which on the whole you did expect) can't be so. I shall in a moment try to say something about the interrelation of these in a typical case.

In contrasting, up to this point, arguments used by metaphysicians with inductive and with deductive arguments, I have spoken as if there were one definite sort of argument that is metaphysical. I think in fact there is no one thing that is a metaphysical argument, just as there is no one thing that is a metaphysical statement. This does not mean, however, that absolutely no general remarks can be made about them; only that such general remarks will serve to characterize these arguments in outline rather than to state some one essential property of them. One essential property of them, however, can be and has been stated: that they are not the same as deductive or inductive arguments. For some philosophers, indeed, such as the so-called logical positivists, this is quite enough; all metaphysical arguments and statements are by them lumped together and dismissed as meaningless. But this skeletal unity tells us nothing about metaphysics; it is only the uniformity of all before the final leveller. The approach of these collectively anti-metaphysical philosophers is a kind of philosophical parallel to the attitude of a fanatically militarist person who divides all men into two classes only, combatants and non-combatants. Even from the military point of view, such a division would have its disadvantages: among non-combatants, for instance, it fails to distinguish between the medically unfit and the conscientious objectors. A metaphysician, in relation to the positivist criterion of meaning, is more like a conscientious objector than like an invalid; it is his whole purpose to do something other than what the positivist wants him to do. And just as there are different kinds of conscientious objector, so there are different types of metaphysician and of metaphysical argument. Understanding can only be gained by taking individual cases.

Within the limits of this chapter it is possible to look at only one example of metaphysical argument in more detail. It has the overwhelming disadvantage of being only one example; but it is such a central and recurrent one that I hope it may yield some general lessons as well.

The stage is set for the argument I am going to consider by the facts of perceptual illusion. All around us we see objects which we recognize as being of certain sorts—trees, tables, people and so on. Occasionally, in the business of recognizing things, we are deceived, and take something that we see for something which in fact it isn't. Thus an old boot in the dusk might be taken for a small cat. Into this setting the philosopher steps. He may be concerned with any of a number of questions, such as 'What do we really know?'; 'How much reliance can be placed on perception as a source of knowledge?'; 'What really exists?'; and so on. But whatever his particular question, his reasoning from the situation of perceptual illusion may well go something like this. 'You were deceived when you took that boot for a cat. Since you were deceived, there can have been no *intrinsic* difference between the experience you had at the moment of seeing what was in fact a boot in the dusk and the experience you could have had in really seeing a cat at that moment. The difference, after all, came out later—when you had a closer look, made a noise, or whatever it was. Clearly there can be no intrinsic difference between the two experiences, for if there were, you could have told the difference, and would not have taken the one thing for the other. So what was this experience you had? Clearly not that of seeing a cat, for there was no cat to be seen. But equally clearly the experience you had wasn't just that of seeing an old boot, either. For we have already agreed that it must have been the same experience as you could have had in really seeing a cat, for otherwise you couldn't have mistaken the boot for a cat; and if you could have had this experience in really seeing a cat, the experience can't just be that of really seeing a boot, for when you really see a cat you don't really see a boot. So the experience you have in both cases must be something neutral between really seeing a cat and really seeing a boot—it is something common to both and less than either. Moreover (this philosopher might continue) 'the having of visual experience must be more basic than the seeing of real objects; for one can have visual experiences without in fact seeing the appropriate, or indeed any, sort of object, but we cannot see an object without having visual experiences.'

So runs the argument from illusion in one of its many forms. It contains both a destructive and a constructive movement; both are typical of metaphysical argument. The destructive movement consists of showing that something we should naturally say if asked to reflect on perception—that is, that we just see objects—is false. It may be said that there is nothing very surprising about this, and that anyone who said that we always, whenever we see anything, see a material object, would obviously be wrong; but that nevertheless we sometimes see material objects. But the destructive movement is stronger than this. The metaphysician does not in fact claim that there is *no* difference between being deceived and not being deceived; his argument is just that the difference is not where you expected it to be. For the argument purports to show that by reflection on the cases of illusion we can come to see that the cases of genuine perception as well are different from what we thought; that in these, too, the visual experience of the observer—which, the metaphysician will go on to argue, is private to the observer—must play a part.

To say this, however, is already to have started the constructive movement of the argument. It is characteristic of metaphysical arguments that the method of destruction already points to what is to take the place of the things destroyed. Hence it is that what is in one sense the same argument—an argument, at any rate, generated by the same facts of experience—can appear in different forms in different philosophers to suit their several purposes. The form in which I have presented the argument from illusion (and some particular form had to be chosen) is in fact one that can lay the foundations for an empiricist metaphysic using the notion of an 'idea' or a 'sensation'.

But the same argument can be used for ends quite different from those of the empiricist metaphysician. Plato, for instance, accepted something like the first stage of the argument, and reasoned from this that our beliefs about the material world must be personal, fleeting and unstable. He added the premisses that true knowledge must be of the unchanging and stable, and that we can up to a point have knowledge, and reached the conclusion that there must be a world of unchanging things, the world of Forms. What he and the empiricists have in common is the use of the argument to destroy a world taken for granted and to substitute something else for it— in his case, a world of Forms, in theirs a succession of experiences from which objects have in some way to be inferred or constructed. Here we see a prime characteristic of metaphysical argument—its use to establish propositions of existence or non-existence. 'The world of Forms is the world of genuine existence'; 'the ultimate constituents of the world are sense-data': these are (very different) metaphysical statements a main prop of which is the argument we have been examining.

How is this argument related to the distinction between inductive and deductive arguments? Clearly it is not just inductive: the empiricist metaphysician, for instance, is not just saying 'there are illusions, so probably objects don't exist and individual experiences do'. Yet he is making a movement beyond what he started with. By examining the concept of perceptual illusion, he arrives at a general conclusion about perception as such; a conclusion which is to be attacked, not by the production of any straightforward empirical counter-examples, but by an enquiry into his concepts, in particular the rather dubious concept of 'an experience'.

'Well', someone might say, 'all we have in this argument is a contingent fact and a set of deductions. The deductions are made from the concept of a perceptual illusion; the contingent fact is that the concept has application—that is, we are sometimes deceived.' But this would be a complete misunderstanding. For neither is the supposed contingent fact just a contingent fact, nor are the supposed deductions just deductions. When the metaphysician says, with a disingenuous air of factual simplicity, 'We are sometimes deceived, and take one thing for another', he is not just stating a contingent fact, something that might well be otherwise. All he actually needs for his argument is the logical possibility of misrecognition, the existence of such a concept; and, very roughly, contained in the concept of recognition is the possibility of misrecognition. So long as we have the concept of recognizing things, we must also have that of failing to recognize them. Of course, we might *perhaps* have neither concept; but what our perception would then seem to be is totally obscure. In the relation of recognition and similar concepts to our experience lies a huge philosophical problem. Again, the deductions are not just deductions. If they were, there could scarcely be the disagreement there is with the conclusion; and, again, the metaphysician has acquired from somewhere *en route* a concept with which he did not start out, that of 'an experience'.

Yet the introduction of this concept is not just gratuitous. It seems to be somehow implied in what is already said, to be demanded by the facts as they stand, and one principal aim of the metaphysician's argument is to display the facts so as to show where the demand comes. The purpose of the argument is not just to deduce a conclusion from the facts. It is rather to show that the account of those facts, when we reflect on them, has a hole in it, a hole which is exactly fitted by the metaphysician's special concept. This concept may be one, like that of 'an experience', which exists already in a rough form in our ordinary language, and which the metaphysician takes up, dignifies and refines into a principle of explanation. Alternatively, if he is a very thoroughgoing metaphysician, the concepts he uses in this way may be much more technical and remote from ordinary thinking, like Leibniz's 'monads' or Kant's 'noumenal objects'.

The greatness of a metaphysician, it seems to me, is to be determined by three considerations: how arbitrary his special concepts are, how much they explain, and how much they distort our ordinary thinking. These considerations are not, of course, independent —they are bound up together rather like the design requirements of an aeroplane, where conflicting demands such as minimum weight, maximum capacity and the requirements of safety have to be reconciled by expert designers. The designer of genius gets as near as possible to having the best of all worlds, and so does the metaphysical genius. His concepts will explain a lot, by revealing important analogies between kinds of experience and thought which superficially seem widely different. These analogies must be real ones, and not the product of forced or over-distorting assimilations; and they must not be arbitrary, in the further sense that one must be led to recognize them, and with them the demand for the metaphysician's explanatory concepts, by clear and cogent argument.

But it is the argument that concerns us here, rather than the features of the metaphysician's enterprise when it is completed. Any account of such arguments in a few words is bound to be a caricature, but their standard features can be summarized like this. The metaphysician feels an inconsistency or difficulty or incompleteness in what we naturally tend to think about some feature of our experience, or rather in what seems to be presupposed by what we so think. In resolving this, he will try to show that some concept on which we rely is secondary to, or presupposed by, some other concept which he has introduced or extended from elsewhere. This concept of his may have a special place in the answer to the problem in question (like the empiricists' use of 'experience'), or he may use it widely elsewhere (like Plato's Forms) to solve other problems; the more widely he uses it elsewhere, the more systematic will his philosophy be.

The compulsiveness of his argument will come from his starting with concepts and features of experience which, it seems, must be there if we are to think about our experience at all. His attempt to show that some concept involves a difficulty, or is presupposed by some other concept, will often issue in statements of existence or non-existence. Yet his assertions of existence or non-existence, unlike assertions of either empirical or mathematical existence, are in a sense only comparative. For all metaphysicians agree that appearance, those features of the world which are metaphysically shown to be unreal, must eventually find *some* place in the account of things as they really are. We saw this before in the empiricist's preservation, in a different place, of the ordinary distinction between illusion and genuine perception. Even McTaggart's famous demonstration of the unreality of time (which is both philosophically spectacular and very hard to refute) is preparatory to an account of what it is that really does exist and presents itself to us confusedly as the passage of time. Hence it is that some have seen the metaphysician's activity as primarily one of reallocation: the extension of some favoured concept to a primary place in the account of things at the expense of more familiar concepts.

There is truth in this; yet the choice of such a concept, and the point of its application, is not just arbitrary—and we are left with the problem of why some work so much better than others. Metaphysical arguments are like trees. Their exact position, and their shape, are to a certain extent matters of preference: the metaphysician can choose where exactly to plant them, and how to trim them. But he cannot choose whether they will grow or not; some spots on the conceptual landscape are more fertile than others. If with the positivist axe we chop the trees down, they grow again. If with the Wittgensteinian spade we start digging up the roots, we shall, fascinatedly, go on and on. For even if we dig up one set of roots, there will be, if it was a stout tree, many others. Perhaps digging is the proper philosophical activity at this time—certainly mere pride in having grown a tree larger than anyone else's is no longer enough. But there was something that justified such pride—the knowledge that the metaphysician's green fingers had found the spot where acorns could grow. What spurs on the philosophical digger is the desire to know more. What makes metaphysical trees grow? Why from some features of our experience rather than others do metaphysical arguments spring up? The answer to that question would be the ultimate metaphysical answer.

Bibliography

The boldface numbers in parentheses following an item indicate its specific relevance to the topics of the Introduction; italicized numbers indicate its relevance to reading selections. The boldface letter **p** at the end of a reference indicates that the volume referred to is available in paperback.

Aaron, R. I. *The Theory of Universals*. Oxford: Clarendon, 1952 (**6**; *9, 10.*).

Aristotle, *Metaphysics*, esp. Chs. 10–17 (**6**; *9, 10;* **p**). *Categories*, esp. pp. 2a11–2b17 (**5**; *6–8*).

Ayer, A. J. *The Problem of Knowledge*. New York: St Martin's, 1956 (**2, 3**; *2–4;* **p**). *Logical Positivism*. Glencoe, Ill.: The Free Press, 1959 (**8**; *12*). *Philosophical Essays*. London: Macmillan, 1954. (**2, 3**; *2–4;* **p**).

Baylis, Charles A. "Universals, Communicable Knowledge and Metaphysics," *Journal of Philosophy*, **XLVIII** (1951), pp. 636–644 (**6**; *9, 10*). "The Given and Perceptual Knowledge," *Philosophic Thought in France and the United States*, Buffalo, N.Y.: University of Buffalo Publications in Philosophy, 1950, pp. 443–461 (**3**; *3, 4*). "A Criticism of Lovejoy's Case for Epistemological Dualism," *Philosophy and Phenomenological Research*, **XXIII** (1963), pp. 527–537 (**3**; *3, 4*).

Blanshard, Brand. *The Nature of Thought*. 2 vols. New York: Macmillan, 1940 (**4**; *5*).

Bradley, F. H. *Appearance and Reality*. London: Allen & Unwin, 1925, p. 392; Oxford: Clarendon, 1930 (**4**; *5*).

Broad, C. D. *Mind and Its Place in Nature*. London: Kegan, New York: Harcourt, 1925 (**1, 2, 3**; *1–4;* **p**).

Carnap, R. "Empiricism, Semantics and Ontology," *Revue Internationale de Philosophie*, **IV** (1950), pp. 20–40 (**8**; *12*).

Chisholm, Roderick M. *Perceiving*. Ithaca, N.Y.: Cornell Univ. Press, 1957 (**3**; *3, 4*).

Descartes, René. *Meditations—Selections*. Ralph M. Eaton (ed.). New York: Scribner's, 1927 (**p**).

Hayakawa, Samuel Ichige. *Language in Action*. New York: Harcourt, 1941 (**6**; *9, 10*).

Joachim, H. H. *The Nature of Truth*. Oxford: Clarendon, 1906, p. 11 (**2**; *2*).

Korzybski, A. *Science and Sanity*. Lancaster, Pa., and New York: The International non-Aristotelian Library Publishing Co., 1933 (**6**; *9, 10*).

Leibniz, Gottfried W. v. *Selections*. Philip P. Wiener (ed.). New York: Scribner's, 1951 (**5**; *6–8;* **p**)

McGilvary, E. B. "Relations in General and Universals in Particular," *The Journal of Philosophy*, XXXVI (1939), pp. 5–15; 29–40 (**6**; *9, 10*).

McTaggart, John McTaggart Ellis. *The Nature of Existence*. Cambridge: Cambridge Univ. Press, 1921–27. *Philosophical Studies*. S. V. Keeling (ed.). London: Arnold, 1934 (**4**; *5*).

Passmore, John. *Philosophical Reasoning*. London: Duckworth, 1961 (**10**; *14*; **p**).

Perry, R. B. *Present Philosophical Tendencies*. New York: Longmans, 1921, pp. 319 ff. (**2, 3**; *2–4*).

Plato. *The Republic*. Francis M. Cornford (trans.). New York: Oxford Univ. Press, esp. Bks. VI, VII, and X (**6**; *9–10*; **p**).

Price, H. H. *Perception*. London: Methuen, 1932, 1950 (**3**; *3, 4*).

Royce, Josiah. *Lectures on Modern Idealism*. New Haven: Yale Univ. Press, 1923 (**6**; *9, 10*; **p**). *Essays in Idealism*. J. E. Smith and A. Castell (eds.). Indianapolis: Library of Liberal Arts (**6**; *9, 10*; **p**).

Russell, Bertrand. *The Problems of Philosophy*. Galaxy Books. New York: Oxford Univ. Press, 1959 (**3, 6**; *3, 4, 9, 10*; **p**).

Ryle, Gilbert. *The Concept of Mind*. New York: University Paperbacks, Barnes & Noble, 1949 (**3**; *3, 4*; **p**). *Dilemmas*. New York: Cambridge Univ. Press, 1960 (**3, 5**; *3, 4, 6–8*; **p**).

Sellars, Wilfrid S. "Realism and the New Way of Words," in H. Feigl and W. S. Sellars (eds.) *Readings in Philosophical Analysis*. New York: Appleton, 1949, pp. 424–456 (**3**; *3, 4*).

Stace, W. T. "The Refutation of Realism," in H. Feigl and W. S. Sellars (eds.). *Readings in Philosophical Analysis*. New York: Appleton, 1949, pp. 364–372 (**3**; *3, 4*).

Strawson, Peter F. *Individuals*. London: Methuen, 1959 (**5, 6**; *6–10*; **p**).

Wilson, N. L. "The Identity of Indiscernibles and the Symmetrical Universe," *Mind, N.S.,* LXII (1953), pp. 506–511 (**5**; *6–8*).

Wisdom, John. "Metaphysics and Verification," *Mind*, XLVI (1937), pp. 452–498 (**8**; *12*).